SOMEWHERE ALONG THE LINE

Fifty Years Love of Trains

THE VANISHED SCENE – The magnificent sight–and sound–of hard-working steam locomotives fighting their way up a long, steep gradient.

This was the scene on the Somerset and Dorset on 2nd August 1952 as 2P 4-4-0 No. 40505 and S&D 7F 2-8-0 No. 53804 came storming up past Prestleigh with a heavy north-bound express. Three miles of 1 in 50 lay behind them, but there was still a further five miles to go before they would reach Masbury Summit, 811 feet above sea level.

Today the Somerset and Dorset is but a memory, for nothing remains of this once splendid line that ran for 72 miles from Bath down to Bournemouth.

The music in my heart I bore,
Long after it was heard no more.

William Wordsworth.

SOMEWHERE ALONG THE LINE

Fifty Years Love of Trains

by Ivo Peters B.E.M.

Oxford Publishing Co.

Acknowledgements

Whereas I delight in taking pictures of trains, I have never been very good at keeping detailed notes of the subjects I photograph. As a result, when I had chosen the pictures for this book, I found, in several instances, that I had only the barest particulars of the subject portrayed. Fortunately several of my friends have come to my rescue with information, and for their help, so readily given, I would particularly like to thank Dick Blenkinsop, the Rev. John Brennan, Paul Hitchcock, Norman Lockett, the Rev. Alan Newman, Brian Reed and Dick Riley.

To Dr. Ernst Schmidt of Reinbek I owe a tremendous debt of gratitude for supplying me with much fascinating information concerning engines I photographed in Germany in the late 'twenties. I am only sorry that it has not been possible to include in the captions, more of the information he has so kindly given me.

Once again, I am grateful to Peggy Leitch for typing my manuscript. However, I suspect that this tedious task may have had its amusing moments when some of my more appalling spelling mistakes cropped up!

Finally, a very sincere 'thank you' to three people who, through their constructive criticism and advice, have been of immense help to me during the preparation of this book — my sister Luise Girdlestone, the Rev. John Brennan and Angela O'Shea.

ISBN 0 902888 80 3

A FOULIS-OPC Railway Book

© 1976 Ivo Peters & Oxford Publishing Co.
Reprinted 1988 (twice) and 1989.

Published by:
Haynes Publishing Group
Sparkford, Nr. Yeovil, Somerset. BA22 7JJ

Haynes Publications Inc.
861 Lawrence Drive, Newbury Park, California 91320, USA.

Contents

"Large or small. . . . ." **1.** A diminutive, 1ft. 10¾in. gauge, Hunslet 6 ton 0-4-0 saddle-tank, and – "City of Nottingham", one of Sir William Stanier's magnificent L.M.S. Pacifics which weighed over 105 tons, without the tender.

Introduction

I have loved trains for as long as I can remember, and any steam locomotive, large or small, new or old, has always fascinated me — although, of course, some are much more attractive than others!

My 'devotion' started at the beginning of the 'twenties when my elder sisters would sometimes take their small brother with them to Saltford station on the G.W.R. main line between Bath and Bristol, to watch the trains. The highlight of any such expedition was to see "The Great Bear", at that time Britain's one and only Pacific. I still recall our intense excitement when we realised that the train tearing towards us, was hauled by this huge, magnificent engine. As she thundered through the small station the platform shook and trembled beneath us and we would all take an involuntary step backwards and brace ourselves against the hurricane which followed as the long line of coaches swept past. A year or two later "The Great Bear" suddenly ceased to appear, and I remember the feeling of utter disbelief followed by the stab of sadness when someone told me that she had been withdrawn and was to be scrapped. In fact she was, of course, rebuilt as a 'Castle', but apart from still carrying her old number 111, as far as I was concerned there was nothing left of my beloved "Great Bear" and it took a long time for me to forgive the Great Western for this act of 'vandalism'!

"Although, of course, some are much more attractive than others...."

2.

One of the remarkable Q.1 0-6-0s – an austerity war-time design by O.V.S. Bulleid for the Southern Railway.

3.

Although "beauty is in the eye of the beholder", few would disagree that the Caledonian Single No. 123, immaculate in her sky-blue livery, was one of the most attractive locomotives ever to run on a British railway.

Then in 1925 my Mother gave me a camera for my birthday, and that summer I took my first picture of a train. Although I have been photographing railway scenes for fifty years, I have to admit that the technical side of photography has never really 'bitten' me — detailed discussions on such things as focal lengths and actinic values leave me way out of my depth! For me, one of the greatest pleasures of railway photography has been when I have discovered some enchanting new location, and then set about trying to get the most attractive picture of the scene. Over the years there have been many such scenes which I have longed to 'capture' for all time. One of these was at Grayrigg in Westmorland, and I shall never forget the first time I discovered this location. It was about six o'clock one evening in late April, 1965, and a thunderstorm was building up to the east. In the distance the fells stood out dramatically against a mass of menacing, black thunder clouds, whilst nearer at hand the silver birches and fresh green larch trees behind Grayrigg signal box shone vividly in the low evening sunlight. The whole scene was superb. On such occasions I have often longed that I had been blessed with the talent of a great artist: however, in the total absence of any such blessing, the use of a camera was the only means of trying to preserve the memory of such an experience.

"The rebuilding of the Southern Bulleid Pacifics, which completely transformed their appearance...."

4.

One of the large Bulleid "Merchant Navy" Pacifics in original condition. No. 35003 "Royal Mail" running at high speed east of Axminster with an up express.

5.

A rebuilt "Merchant Navy", No. 35008 "Orient Line", approaching Bournemouth Central with the 10.08 a.m. Bournemouth West to Waterloo.

Although the number of railway photographs I have taken since 1925 is something over 12,000 the major proportion of the pictures I have chosen for this book were taken after the Second World War. There are two reasons for this. Firstly, the lenses in my pre-war cameras were not of high quality, and pictures from my pre-war negatives are not really suitable for reproduction. Secondly, there is a gap from 1934 until after the Second World War during which time I took hardly any railway pictures. This was because whilst up at Cambridge in the early 'thirties I had become 'hooked' on motor racing, and on coming down from the University all my spare time was devoted to this extremely exhilarating and exciting sport. So, although I never lost my love of trains, sadly I have very few railway pictures taken in the late 'thirties.

In the fifty years that have passed since I photographed my first train there have been many and far-reaching changes in Britain's railways. I have shared in the excitement at the first appearance of a new class of locomotive, such as the famous Great Western "Kings", and 36 years later, have watched with sadness as the last of this class passed by on her final run. In contrast, in more recent times I have seen diesel types, such as the Western Region "Warships", come and go in a mere decade. But as these engines cost some £120,000 each, as a taxpayer I prefer not to dwell on this! On a happier note, there have been many engine 'events' which interested me greatly, such as the rebuilding of the Southern Bulleid Pacifics, which completely transformed their appearance — much to my approval!

As a change from engine matters, in the early 'thirties I watched the building of the new section of main line to bypass Frome; and in recent years I have seen the magnificent and once thriving Southern main line west of Salisbury, singled and reduced to near impotence.

"The excitement at the first appearance of a new engine — and the sadness of the final run...."

6.

July 1928. Great Western "King" class 4-6-0 No. 6018 "King Henry VI", just one month old, standing in Bath station with the 6.30p.m. down express from Paddington. This was one of the first appearances of a "King" at Bath. For the initial nine months of their existence, the class were barred from running through Bath until a bridge, just to the west of the station, had been strengthened.

7.

April 1963. No. 6018, the final "King" to remain in service, makes her last appearance in charge of a Stephenson Locomotive Society special to Swindon.

Photo courtesy
The Irish Times.

8. Motor racing — *"This extremely exhilarating and exciting sport"*, that lured me away from railway photography in the 'thirties.

This is the start of the Limerick Grand Prix in August, 1936, a 150 mile "Round the houses" race — 55 laps of a 2¾ mile circuit — held in the heart of the city. We were started in two groups. I was in the second group — car No. 22 — seen here just after the start.

With less than three miles to go, and when lying 3rd, my engine blew up with an almighty bang. Motor racing could bring the height of elation — or the depth of misery!

And so to the fateful 'sixties, and the opening of the floodgates of modernisation and rationalisation. Everywhere the railway scene was one of change, but even so, the latter half of the decade saw two events which, but a few years earlier, I would have thought utterly impossible. In 1966 my beloved Somerset and Dorset line — the whole 72 miles from Bath to Bournemouth — was abandoned and torn up. And in 1968 the use of steam locomotives by British Railways came to an end. At the time, with the two main props of my railway enthusiasm lost, I wondered whether my life-long love of trains would survive. I am happy to say that it has.

Tempora mutantur, nos et mutamur in illis.

BATH,
SOMERSET.

IVO PETERS
1976

9.

'N' class 2-6-0 No. A864 arriving at Mortehoe station with a local from Ilfracombe.

PART 1

In the Beginning – 1925

I took my first picture of a train in 1925. That summer my Mother gave me a camera for my birthday, and shortly after this 'event' we all set off for a family holiday at Woolacombe in North Devon. I was allowed to travel down by train, a decision which I suspect my Mother regretted slightly for as a result I discovered that Mortehoe, the station for Woolacombe, was less than two miles from where we were staying — and I spent more time at the station than on the beach!

MORTEHOE

Mortehoe, on the line between Barnstaple and Ilfracombe, lay at the top of a terrific bank, the railway climbing for 5¾ miles, largely at 1 in 37. After passing through the station, the line descended, equally precipitously, towards Ilfracombe.

During my visit in August, 1925, many of the trains were being worked by 'N' class 2-6-0s. These were interesting engines, for although the original design was by Maunsell for the South Eastern and Chatham Railway, they had been built at Woolwich Arsenal in 1920/2 on orders from the Government, to alleviate post-war unemployment. Twenty were purchased by the Southern Railway in 1924 and a further thirty in 1925. They came under the Eastern section of the Southern Railway for numbering, carrying the letter A (for Ashford) above the number.

Because of the severity of the climb up to Mortehoe, most trains of over three coaches had an assisting engine, usually an M7 0-4-4 tank.

10.

'N' class 2-6-0 No. A860 and M7 0-4-4T. No. E48, standing in Mortehoe station with a train bound for Ilfracombe. The M7 was a Western section engine, the E before her number being for Eastleigh.

THE LYNTON AND BARNSTAPLE RAILWAY

One day I caught a local train from Mortehoe to Barnstaple to go for a ride on the Lynton and Barnstaple Railway. This was a delightful, 19 mile, narrow gauge line opened in 1898 to connect the seaside resorts of Lynton and Lynmouth with Barnstaple. The gauge was 1ft. 11½in. and the terminus at Barnstaple was alongside the L. & S.W.R. (later Southern Railway) up platform at Barnstaple Town Station. There were five locomotives, four 2-6-2Ts built by Manning, Wardle, and one 2-4-2T. by Baldwin.

The Lynton and Barnstaple was taken over by the Southern Railway in 1923, but it was not a paying proposition, and twelve years later the line was closed and demolished – a sad end to a delightful little railway which, had it survived until after the Second World War, could well have become one of the leading preserved 'leisure lines' of today.

11 and 12   "Exe", one of the 2-6-2Ts built by Manning, Wardle in 1897, works No. 1362.

13.   "Lyn", the 2-4-2T built by Baldwin in 1897, works No. 15965. She was of typical American appearance, having a large wooden cab, two dome-shaped sand boxes on top of the boiler, and cow-catchers front and rear.

BATH ROAD SHED, BRISTOL,
September, 1925.

14. On shed in this view are — a "County" class 4-4-0, behind which is a "Star" class 4-6-0 and, standing alongside the "Star", a "Bulldog" class 4-4-0.

One afternoon in early September 1925 I was standing on the platform at the western extremity of Temple Meads station, Bristol, looking longingly over towards the engine sheds, when I noticed an official-looking, bowler-hatted, gentleman approaching. So I plucked up courage and asked if I could be allowed to walk over to the sheds to take a picture. I was in luck, for after a brief pause whilst he eyed me shrewdly, my bowler-hatted friend said "Yes, sonny; but you will have to look sharp about it. Come with me!" This was my first visit to an engine shed, and I bubbled over with excitement. Never before had I been in such close proximity with engines; from rail-level they seemed so much bigger, and to tower above me.

After three rather hasty pictures, I was escorted back to the platform by my friend to whom I expressed my profuse thanks. Although my 'visit' had lasted less than five minutes, it had been a tremendous thrill, and for days afterwards I could talk of nothing else.

Right up to the end of steam, over forty years later, this sense of excitement whenever I visited an engine shed, never left me.

Photographs of Bath Road Shed, taken thirty-four years later, in 1959, appear in pictures 373 to 377.

15. A head-on view of "Star" class 4-cylinder 4-6-0 No. 4063 "Bath Abbey".

16. An 'open-cab' pannier tank 0-6-0 heads a "Star" class 4-6-0 on the coal stage road at Bath Road Shed, Bristol, in September, 1925.

BRISTOL, 1925.

17. One of the G.W.R. "Saint" class 2-cylinder 4-6-0s, No. 2954 "Tockenham Court", standing at the western end of Temple Meads station with a down local.

BATH, 1925.

18. The G.W.R. built many varieties of 4-4-0. This is one of the "Flower" class which had coupled wheels of 6ft. 8½in. No. 4165 "Narcissus" is running into Bath station with a down express in July 1925. She had entered service in July 1908 and was withdrawn in July 1927, two years after this picture was taken.

19.

Evening departure.
A down local sets off from Saltford behind an elderly 4-4-0

SALTFORD STATION, 1925.

From my home in the village of Corston, it was a pleasant one-mile walk, mostly across fields, to Saltford
station on the G.W.R. main line between Bath and Bristol.
Here I spent innumerable happy hours watching the
trains. The station master, Mr. Redwood, was a kindly
man who appreciated my deep interest in railways and
used to give me long discourses on various aspects of railway operation. Occasionally I would be allowed to spend
a brief period in the signal box where one of the signal-
men, Mr. Potter, explained to me the basic details of the
signalling system. Very early on I had copied into my note
book the G.W.R. bell-code which I took upon myself as
a matter of honour to learn by heart!

20.

Morning spectacle.
A "Saint" class 4-6-0 approaching the station at high speed with an up Bristol-Paddington express.

21.

One of the Great Western steam rail motors passes by on her way to Bath. Introduced in 1903 for local services, these had the outward appearance of a normal coach, but the bogie at one end was in fact a small steam engine with cylinders 12in. x 16in., outside Walschaerts valve gear, and a vertical boiler. The last of these steam rail motors was withdrawn from service in 1935.

The Great Western main line passed by only one field away from the bottom of my garden. The speed of most express trains at this spot defeated my photographic attempts, but I had more luck with up local trains which were only just starting to gather speed after their stop at Saltford.

22.

Another east-bound local, but this time composed of two coaches drawn by an 0-4-2 tank engine.

23.

One of the "Duke" class 4-4-0s, designed by William Dean in 1895 heading east in charge of an up train.

PART 2
To Germany for the Summer Holidays, 1926 -29

1925 was destined to be the last time we would all spend a summer holiday together as a family for, very sadly, that autumn my Mother died.

As the 1926 summer holidays drew near, my Father announced that he was going to take me to the Harz Mountains in Germany. Of course the prospect of this 'expedition' excited me tremendously, the more so since we were going to travel by train, catching the "Hook Continental" from Liverpool Street and sailing on the night boat from Parkeston Quay to the Hook of Holland.

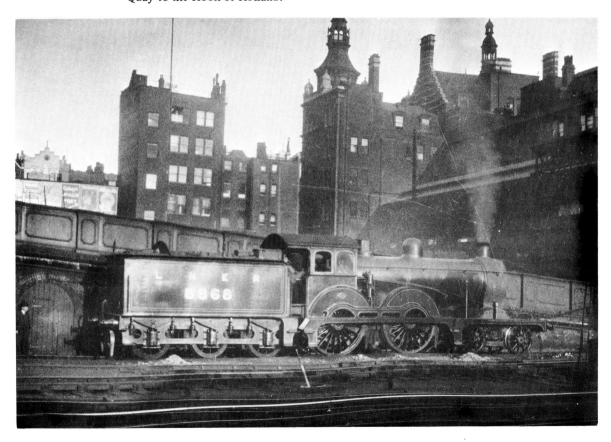

LIVERPOOL STREET

24 and 25. Liverpool Street — the London terminus of the old Great Eastern Railway, on a fine evening in early August, 1926. This was my first view of James Holden's graceful "Claud Hamilton" 4-4-0s. No. 8868, built in 1903, was one of the early engines of this class which had a round-topped firebox. The other 4-4-0 is a later development of the design with a Belpaire firebox.

No. 8868, in L.N.E.R. apple-green livery, and fully lined-out, looked an absolute picture in the early evening light.

26. No. 8504, one of the '1500' class 4-6-0s which first appeared in 1912. In contrast to the 4-4-0s, No. 8504 had not yet been repainted in L.N.E.R. livery, and was in plain unlined grey, with just her number in large numerals on the tender.

27. The summer holiday in Germany in 1926 had set a pattern for further visits, and in August, 1928, my Father and I were once again at Liverpool Street on our way to Germany for a holiday in the Harz Mountains.

On this occasion, Liverpool Street produced an interesting engine for me in the form of an ex-G.N.R. 2-6-0, No. 4694.

28.
4-6-0 No. 3507 basking in the early morning sunshine at the Hook of Holland in August, 1926. There were only eight engines of this class. The first six, Nos. 3501-3506, were built in 1908 by Beyer, Peacock & Co. No. 3507 followed later in 1914 and was constructed in Germany by Hohenzollern A.G. für Lokomotivbau.

HOLLAND, 1926.

Although I had seen pictures of Dutch engines, and knew that they were painted green, I was not really fully prepared for the sight that met my eyes at the Hook of Holland that morning in early August, 1926, for at the end of the platform, and simmering gently, stood an absolutely magnificent 4-6-0 resplendent in fresh green livery and with her copper and brass fittings glinting in the early morning sunshine. I thought it was one of the most beautiful engines I had ever seen.

There was just time for one rather rushed picture before my Father shepherded me towards our train and the Mitropa coach in which we were to travel across Holland and as far as Hannover in Germany. In charge of the Mitropa service, and waiting to welcome us at the entrance to the coach, was Herr Schneider, an old friend of my Father's, who showed us to our reserved compartment. This was totally different from any English compartment in which I had ever travelled, being in effect a very comfortable small room complete with arm chairs and a sofa. There was one large window which, somewhat to my Father's growing perturbation, I frantically lowered at frequent intervals in my attempts to photograph engines standing outside sheds as we passed by.

29. As we were pulling out of one station, this most attractive, elderly 0-6-0 suddenly came into view standing in an adjacent platform. One glimpse of her chimney and dome was sufficient to show that she had been built by Beyer, Peacock & Co. The first four of this class appeared in 1865 and further batches continued to be built up to 1878.

30. A cautious approach to another large station gave me the opportunity to take this side view of 4-4-0 No. 1934, her highly polished brass dome gleaming in the early morning sunshine. She was one of a class of forty locomotives, and entered service in 1912. Just in the picture on the right hand side is an equally immaculate 0-6-0T.

31. Standing outside one shed as we passed by was this handsome 4-6-0. She was a 4-cylinder engine and one of a large class numbered from 3701 to 3820. The design originated in 1910 and over the next 18 years successive batches were built by several different manufacturers.

32. As we swept past another shed, I attempted this shot — into the sun — of a 2-4-0 and a 4-4-0 standing facing each other. Once again, there was no mistaking the origin of the 2-4-0 whose chimney and dome were pure Beyer, Peacock. She was in fact one of 179 engines, numbered from 1301 to 1479, built over a period of 15 years from 1880 to 1895. The 4-4-0, No. 1818, was also built by Beyer, Peacock and entered service in 1906.

33. On our 1928 holiday, when the time came for the Dutch to hand over our train to the Germans, I was intrigued to find, on leaning out of the window, that we were being hauled by one of the large German class 01 2-cylinder Pacifics. On my first visit to Germany in 1926 I had seen only one of these impressive giants.

GERMANY, 1926/28.

A series of pictures taken from the train.

34.   At one stage we rapidly overtook this goods train coming in on a converging line.

35. Another attempted engine shed shot 'against the light'. This time the engine was an ex-Prussian class P8 4-6-0 No. 38 2872, which had been built by Vulcan, Stettin, in 1921, maker's number 3629.

Before my first visit to Germany in 1926, I had been under the impression that the 0-10-0 "Lickey Banker" was a remarkable, if not unique, engine. So it came as a bit of a shock to find that in Germany, 0-10-0s were "Two a penny"!

36. We sweep past an ex-Prussian class T16 0-10-0T, No. 94 392, in charge of a goods train. No. 94 392 was built by Schwartzkopf, Berlin, in 1912, maker's number 4905.

37. Looking nonchalantly out of the window on one occasion, I was suddenly delighted to see the tail-end of another train come into view as we began to overhaul a goods train running parallel with us on an adjacent track. So down came the window and I leant out (far too far for my Father's happiness!) to get this picture of 0-10-0 No. 57 3135 at the head of her train. No. 57 3135, an ex-Prussian class G10, was built by Hanomag, Hannover, in 1922, maker's number 10068.

38. No. 57 2462, another ex-Prussian class G10 0-10-0 was engaged in some shunting as we passed by.

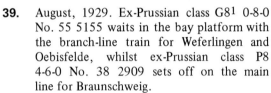

HELMSTEDT, 1926-29.

39. August, 1929. Ex-Prussian class G8¹ 0-8-0 No. 55 5155 waits in the bay platform with the branch-line train for Weferlingen and Oebisfelde, whilst ex-Prussian class P8 4-6-0 No. 38 2909 sets off on the main line for Braunschweig.

ANCIENT — AND MODERN.

40.

Interesting power for a west-bound local. In August 1926 ex-Prussian class T9³ 2-6-0T. No. 91 541, running bunker-first, is coupled ahead of elderly ex-Prussian class P4² compound 4-4-0 No. 36 070, a type first introduced in 1892.

42. ▶

One of the very impressive Class 01 2-cylinder Pacifics, No. 01 039, pauses briefly at Helmstedt in August, 1928 with a Berlin-Hannover express. At the time of this picture, No. 01 039 was less than one year old. Built by Henschel, Kassel, in 1927, maker's number 20842, she was allocated to Magdeburg Depot and entered service on 7th January, 1928.

41. On one of our journeys in August, 1926, we had quite a time to wait at Helmstedt, so whilst I stayed at the station to watch the trains, my Father went into the town to do some shopping. After taking one or two photographs at the eastern end of the station I wandered along the platform and found at the western end an ex-Prussian class G10 0-10-0, No. 57 2121 coupled to a tank wagon standing up against the buffers in the bay platform. Ah, I thought, an excellent opportunity to photograph one of these interesting engines. The tank wagon was emitting curious gurgling noises and periodic wafts of steam which drifted down over the engine, so I waited to pick (I hoped) the right moment to "press the button". The crew of the engine had now become aware that they were to be photographed, and called across to some station staff standing on the platform, whereupon they all looked at me and burst into uproarious laughter. This was somewhat off-putting. (Which is my excuse for having cut off the bottom of the front wheels of the engine.) Regrettably I couldn't speak any German and so did not know what had been said. However, at this precise moment my Father appeared on the scene and observing the general merriment, spoke to one of the station staff, whereupon he also burst out laughing. What, I asked somewhat petulantly, was so funny about my taking a picture of an interesting engine? To which my Father replied that whereas the engine might well be interesting, what, in fact, I had just photographed with such care was a railborne sewage disposal unit busily engaged in pumping out the gents' lavatory.

43. Evening departure. As the light began to fade one evening in early August, 1926, 4-6-0 No. 38 3343 set off eastwards with an express for Berlin.

44. Morning call. Many of the more important trains passing through Helmstedt in 1929 were hauled by ex-Prussian class P10 2-8-2s. No. 39 149, in charge of an express from Berlin, was just getting her train under way again for the run to Braunschweig. She was built in 1924 by Henschel, Kassel, maker's number 20190, and had a life of 42 years, being scrapped in 1966.

45. In August, 1926 one of the engines engaged in shunting the yard at Helmstedt was this ex-Prussian class T11 2-6-0T. No. 74 317, a type first built in 1903.

46. One of the trains I photographed prior to the "Tank wagon episode" — see picture 41 — was an east-bound express hauled by this interesting large ex-Prussian class S6 4-4-0, No. 13 1238. 581 of these engines were built between 1906 and 1913.

47. Ex-Prussian class P8 4-6-0 No. 38 1667 standing outside Helmstedt engine shed — a picture taken in 1926, before the fitting of smoke deflectors became the 'in thing' for locomotives. The class P8 4-6-0s were one of the most famous types of steam locomotive on the continent of Europe. 3561 of these very capable and versatile engines were built for German railways, and many more were sold for service in other European countries including Poland, Romania and Lithuania.

No. 38 1667 was built in 1914 by Berliner Maschinebau — Act. Ges., maker's number 2438.

48. On the journey through Holland we had to cross over the Rhine on a car-ferry, and just up stream was a most impressive bridge carrying the railway over the river. When we were about halfway across, what I had hoped for, happened — a long goods train passed slowly over the bridge.

HOLLAND, 1929.

I had not been back at school long at the start of the summer term in 1929, when I received a letter from my Father saying that he was making arrangements for us to visit the Harz Mountains again for the summer holidays, but on this occasion we would be travelling by road. My first reaction was one of disappointment — no evening of eager anticipation at Liverpool Street, no early morning atmosphere of excitement at the Hook of Holland. As it turned out, however, travelling by road had its compensations, for although I saw far fewer engines, I did see my first Dutch steam tram.

49. After passing through one town, I noticed that we had some tram lines running beside the road, and in the distance ahead, to my great excitement, there appeared a smudge of smoke — we were catching up with a steam-hauled tram! The exact point at which we overhauled the tram was on a level-crossing over a main line, which meant that I had to attempt a rather 'bumpy' shot from the car, as my Father was disinclined to stop at this stage in the journey

50. As a part of our holiday in 1929, we were spending a couple of days in Holland. On the first evening we had gone out from our hotel after dinner for a stroll along a canal bank beside which ran some rusty rails. Rounding a bend, we suddenly came upon this marvellous, and totally unexpected, sight — a small 0-4-0 well-tank in charge of half-a-dozen wagons, resting under some trees. There wasn't enough light for a photograph but nevertheless I "had a go" and got this under-exposed picture to remind me of this happy occasion.

GERMANY, 1929.

51. A sad fact, but one I had to accept, was that my Father had no interest in railways, and so it was quite a 'battle' to get him to stop the car for a picture of a train. (He used to ration me to about four "railway picture stops" per journey!) However, on this occasion he had no choice but to stop as this elderly German 0-6-0 made her way across the road in front of us with some equally ancient coaches.

52. Another picture taken from the car on the move. This diminutive 0-4-0 well-tank was engaged in some road reconstruction work in the Harz Mountains.

THE HARZ MOUNTAINS.

The Nordhausen, Wernigerode Railway was a fascinating metre
gauge line which ran through the Harz Mountains to connect Wernigerode in the north with Nordhausen in the south. From Drei
Annen-Hohne a branch diverged from the main line to climb, via
Schierke, up to the top of the Brocken, 1142 metres above sea
level, the highest mountain in the Harz. As might be expected for
a railway that abounded in steep gradients and sharp curves, most
of the locomotives were Mallet Articulated 0-4-4-0 tanks, with two
larger 2-4-4-2 Mallets, Nos. 51 and 52, used mainly on the Brocken
trains.

54.

In the latter half of the twenties, the largest engines owned
by the N.W.R. were two
2-4-4-2 Mallet tanks Nos. 51
and 52. These were used
mainly on the Brocken trains
and when I took this picture
of No. 51 standing at Schierke
in August, 1926, she was
four years old, having been
built by Borsig in 1922,
maker's number 11382.

◄ 53. For our holidays in the Harz Mountains we always went to Schierke and the hotel Fürst zu Stolberg, one of the most pleasant and comfortable hotels in which I have ever stayed. Travelling to Schierke by train, one had to change at Wernigerode from the main line to the narrow gauge, but this was a simple matter as the terminus of the Nordhausen, Wernigerode Railway lay just to the rear of the main line station. On our holiday in August, 1928, we found 0-4-4-0T. No. 11 standing in the station with our train for Schierke. No. 11 was built by Jung in 1897, maker's number 258.

55. A lucky shot of one of the 0-4-4-0 Mallets running into Schierke with a train bound for the Brocken. A fraction of a second after 'pressing the button' my view of the engine was totally obscured by a vast lady stepping in front of me!

56. Another of the 0-4-4-0 Mallets arriving at the terminus on top of the Brocken on a gloomy day in August, 1928.

59. One fine afternoon in late August, 1928, we set off from Schierke for the six-kilometre walk through the forest to Drei Annen-Hohne, a small hamlet, and the junction for the branch line that climbed, via Schierke, to the top of the Brocken. On arriving at Drei Annen-Hohne we adjourned to a small hotel for refreshment, and were served with coffee by an extremely attractive blonde waitress. The coffee was excellent, and I decided I would like a second cup, whereupon a friend of my Father's who was with us, said I should ask for it myself — it was high time I started to learn some German. So he told me the German for "Give me another cup please", and when the waitress next appeared, I beamed upon her and said "Geben Sie mir ein Küss bitte". The result was dramatic! Even to this day, the memory of what took place is somewhat embarrassing! Needless to say, my Father and his friend thought it was a huge joke.

In the early evening, we caught a train back to Schierke and as we departed from Drei Annen-Hohne I took this picture — from the rear verandah of the last coach — of 0-4-4-0T. No. 14 waiting to leave with a train for Nordhausen.

57. A view taken from the open verandah of the end coach as our train descended towards Wernigerode in August, 1928. This gives some indication of the sinuous path often followed by the line as it hugged the mountainside.

58.

Amongst the attractions of a holiday in the Harz mountains were the walks through the dense pine forests. It could be a boiling hot summer's day, but in the heart of the forest it would be cool, peaceful and utterly still.

Now and again on these walks we would suddenly come upon the railway, which had been laid through the forest with a minimum of disturbance. We had not realised we were anywhere near the line, when these two 0-4-4-0 Mallets, Nos. 12 and 13, suddenly appeared running quietly downhill through the forest.

60.

0-6-0T. No. 6 waiting in the loop at Schierke station in August, 1926, whilst on her way up to the Brocken in connection with some engineering work. This locomotive was originally ordered for the Prussian Army Technical Research Establishment. She was built in 1914 by Henschel, maker's number 12879.

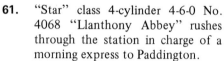

61. "Star" class 4-cylinder 4-6-0 No. 4068 "Llanthony Abbey" rushes through the station in charge of a morning express to Paddington.

PART 3

The Early 'Thirties

SALTFORD STATION.

Saltford station, my 'happy hunting ground' for over 40 years, was 4½ miles west of Bath on the Great Western main line from Paddington to Bristol. Over the years, I spent innumerable happy hours here; but never again, for this little country station is now but a memory. Station buildings, platforms, signal box, small goods yard — all have been swept away under British Railway's modernisation programme, and today no trace remains of this once pleasant little country station.

62.

One of William Dean's elderly but excellent 0-6-0s approaching with an up goods.

63. Leading to the station on the up side was a footpath which ran right beside the line, but slightly below track-level. This was a tremendously exciting place from which to watch the trains, especially the expresses, which would thunder past literally only a few feet away from one. This picture of a "Saint" class 2-cylinder 4-6-0 heading west at high speed with a down express, was taken from this footpath.

64. Another "Star" class 4-6-0 draws near with an afternoon express from Paddington to Bristol.

65. "King" class 4-cylinder 4-6-0 No. 6001 "King Edward VII" pauses briefly with a down local in the summer of 1932. At that time, Mr. C.B. Collett, the Great Western C.M.E., was anxious to find out just how fast the "Kings" could travel, and this engine had been fitted temporarily with a speedometer. Part of the equipment for this can just be seen in this picture, including the rod from the right-hand rear coupled wheel, and the cable leading up to a box fitted to the outside of the cab just to the rear of the side window.

Twenty one years later, I was to see this same engine engaged in some most interesting Controlled Road Tests. See pictures 194 to 196.

SALTFORD STATION.

66. During a morning session watching trains at Saltford, one of the things to which I used to look forward, was the arrival of the pick-up goods from Bristol. On this occasion the train was being worked by a "Bulldog" class 4-4-0. The Great Western built 156 of these most competent and useful engines, which had coupled wheels of 5ft. 8ins.

67. I remember well the excitement in 1923 when, with a flourish of publicity, the Great Western brought out the first of their new 4-cylinder "Castle" class engines. This was No. 4073, "Caerphilly Castle", which is now preserved in the Science Museum, London. She is seen here in 1932 setting off from Saltford station in charge of a stopping train to Bristol.

68. Another "Bulldog" class 4-4-0, No. 3378 "River Tawe", coasting in with a down local.

69.
Southern D15 class 4-4-0 No. 472 passing through Saltford in charge of the morning express from Portsmouth to Bristol. The D15 class, of which there were 10 engines, came out in 1912-13 and was Dugald Drummond's last design before he died.

A sight in the early 'thirties to which I always looked forward was the through-working of Southern engines over the Great Western on Portsmouth-Bristol trains. This produced an interesting variety of ex-London and South Western Drummond 4-4-0s.

70. The morning Portsmouth-Bristol express, this time composed of Southern stock and hauled by a Southern L12 4-4-0. There were 20 engines in this class which was introduced in 1904-5. With their high-pitched boiler and Urie chimney (a later fitting) I always thought of them as ungainly engines. It was an L12 that was involved in the ghastly accident at Salisbury in 1906.

One of the T9s — a class for which I had great affection — passes by at speed. The train is composed of Great Western stock with a clerestory coach next to the engine. 66 of Drummond's T9 class were built between 1899 and 1901; they were outstandingly good locomotives, and were known as "greyhounds".

72. One of the impressive "King" class 4-cylinder 4-6-0s heading east with a Bristol – Paddington express.

There were two railways almost at the bottom of my garden -

THE GREAT WESTERN –

The Paddington-Bristol main line passed by just one field away.

73.

On warm summer evenings I often used to stroll down to the bottom of the garden after dinner to watch the 6.30 express from Paddington pass by. One evening in early July, 1933, I walked across the field to take this picture of the train, hauled by a "Castle" class engine. Had I been more interested in the technical side of photography I probably would not have "pressed the button", for it was after half past eight and there was not really sufficient light for a photograph.

Luckily, however, this did not occur to me – and so I have this picture to remind me of a happy evening 43 years ago.

74. A very lucky 'snap' shot! In the early 'thirties "Saint" class engines were a common sight on the Bristol main line. Whilst out for a walk one day in August, 1932, I stopped to watch an express approaching, thinking ". . . just another "Saint" ". Suddenly, however it dawned on me that this "Saint" was different – and my camera was still in its case! Somehow I managed to get it out just in the nick of time to obtain this interesting, but decidedly indifferent, picture of "Saint" class 4-6-0 No. 2935 "Caynham Court" which had been fitted experimentally with Lentz R.C. poppet valve gear. A few days later I saw this engine again, standing in Bath station. See picture 86.

75. Ex-Midland 2P 4-4-0 No. 526 and a Johnson 0-4-4T. running between Kelston and Bitton with a local bound for Bristol.

and THE LONDON MIDLAND AND SCOTTISH

Less than a ¼ mile to the north, and running parallel with the Great Western, was the Mangotsfield-Bath branch of the former Midland Railway.

Because of severe weight restrictions imposed by a series of weak bridges — the Midland crossed over the river Avon no less than six times in the first 5 miles between Bath and Bitton — the largest passenger engines permitted over this line in the early 'thirties were the ex-M.R. and L.M.S. class 2P 4-4-0s. Local trains were hauled mainly by ex-Midland Johnson 0-4-4 tanks. By 1938 all the bridges had been strengthened and from then on almost any L.M.S. engine was permitted to work down to Bath. See pictures 422 and 423.

76. Most goods trains were hauled by either 3F or 4F 0-6-0s. This picture of a 3F-hauled goods was taken some 2 miles west of Bath — where a public footpath most obligingly crossed the line.

77.

For very many years the ex-Midland Johnson 0-4-4 tanks virtually monopolised the working of the local passenger service over the branch, until superseded in the late 'forties by Stanier's 2-6-2, and 0-4-4 tanks. This train was in the charge of Johnson tank No. 1309, still in her original condition with Salter valves on the dome, and a round topped firebox. For more views of these engines, see pictures 79, 145, 236 and 237.

THE L.M.S. STATION AT BATH.*

This terminus, known as 'Queen Square' until the railways were nationalised, when it became 'Green Park', was built by the Midland Railway in 1869. It was also used by the Somerset and Dorset, whose trains joined the Midland line at Bath Junction for the ½ mile run into the terminus.

78. A pair of 0-6-0s, ex-S & D 3F No. 3228 and a 4F, reversing out from the station after bringing in an express over the Somerset and Dorset from Bournemouth.

79. Ex-Midland Johnson 0-4-4T. No. 1391 stands in the middle road, coupled to a Midland clerestory coach. No. 1391 had been rebuilt with a Belpaire firebox, closed dome and pop safety valves.

Illustrated in considerable detail in my book "The Somerset and Dorset, an English Cross-Country Railway", published by the Oxford Publishing Company.

80. One of the high-lights of a visit to the L.M.S. station at Bath was to see the "Pines Express" which ran between Manchester and Bournemouth. Queen Square Station was a terminus, so one had the added interest of seeing the "Pines Express" arrive behind one engine, and then set off again hauled by another engine which had coupled on at the other end. In this view, the up "Pines Express" is standing in the station after the run from Bournemouth, and ex-Midland 2P 4-4-0 No. 518 has just coupled on for the continuation of the run North.

81. Ex-Midland 2P 4-4-0 No. 377 waiting to depart with the down "Pines Express" for the run over the Somerset and Dorset down to Bournemouth. The fireman has not yet placed in position the tablet catcher, ready for the single-line section that lies ahead between Bath Junction and Midford.

THE L.M.S. SHEDS AT BATH.*

This motive power depot was composed of the old Midland shed and the much larger Somerset and Dorset shed.

82. Leading this line-up is ex-Midland Johnson 2-4-0 No. 157, built in 1876. Behind her are two standard L.M.S. engines, a 2P 4-4-0 and a 3F 0-6-0T. It is interesting to compare this Johnson-designed 2-4-0 which had inside frames, with Kirtley's earlier design with outside frames, as shown in picture 418.

83. Ex-Midland 2P 4-4-0 No. 495. This was one of the numerous '483' class originally built by Johnson in 1882-1901, but later extensively rebuilt first by Deeley, and then by Fowler.

Bath Motive Power Depot is profusely illustrated in my book "The Somerset and Dorset – an English Cross-Country Railway", published by the Oxford Publishing Company.

THE "PINES EXPRESS".*

During the summer months this was often a very heavy train and was hauled by pairs of 2P 4-4-0s, weight limitations imposed by weak bridges precluding the use of more powerful locomotives.

84. A pair of ex-Midland 2P 4-4-0s drawing near to Bath with the down "Pines Express". This shot was taken from a public footpath right-of-way over the line some 2 miles west of Bath. (See pictures 76 and 77). On this occasion I had, unfortunately, misjudged the time, and the train and I arrived more or less simultaneously at the crossing — hence this very indifferent picture.

85. 2P 4-4-0s, working in double-harness, would often also be in charge of the train over the Somerset and Dorset. Here a pair of ex-Midland 2Ps are starting the 1 in 50 climb out of Bath over the single-line section to Midford.

Many illustrations of the "Pines Express" during the period 1948-62 appear in my book "The Somerset and Dorset — an English Cross-Country Railway" published by the Oxford Publishing Company.

86. "Saint" class 4-6-0 No. 2935 "Caynham Court", fitted experimentally with Lentz R.C. poppet valve gear, stands in the station with an up express in August 1932. For another view of this engine, see picture 74.

THE G.W.R. STATION, BATH.

87. An event always interesting to watch was the arrival at Bath of the "One o'clock slip". In this shot, the slip portion has parted company with the main train and the guard in charge of the slip is preparing to bring his coaches to a stand in the down platform. As soon as the passengers had disembarked, a strategically placed Pannier Tank would remove the slip coaches from the main line. The G.W.R. was the leading protagonist in the art of slip coach working.

88.
In the 'thirties there were through workings of Southern engines over the G.W.R. on Portsmouth-Bristol trains. One of Drummond's 4-4-0 designs for the L. & S.W.R., D15 class No. 472, prepares to set off from Bath with a return Bristol-Portsmouth train. More of these through workings are illustrated in pictures 69, 70 and 71.

I have always had a particular affection for this large and very busy station, which was used jointly by the G.W.R. and the L.M.S., for it provided me with considerable consolation when I was young.

In the early 'thirties I was nearing the end — thank heaven — of the four most unhappy years of my life, at a school "Not 100 miles from the centre of Bristol". We occasionally had a "free afternoon" when it was permissible to go down into Bristol, and I used to make a bee-line for Temple Meads to try and forget my misery for a couple of hours by watching trains.

89. Ex-Midland 2P 4-4-0 No. 496 standing at the western end of the station. She was piloting a Compound 4-4-0 and they had just arrived with a train from the North.

90. Two G.W.R. engines, a 2-6-0 and a 2-6-2T., bringing in empty stock at the western end of the station.

A RATHER UNUSUAL GREAT WESTERN TYPE

91.

One day during the summer holidays in 1931 I went up to London by train and took this picture of Great Western 2-4-2T. No. 3610 as we were nearing Paddington. It was a type of G.W. engine that I never saw in my "home" territory around Bath and Bristol. This shot — taken through the glass of my compartment window using 1/100th of a second — typifies the outrageous luck I sometimes had with my pictures. I am sure that if I had been more interested in the technical side of photography I would never have attempted it. (Of course I also had — and deservedly so — masses of failures!)

92.
Two of Logan and Hemingway's Manning Wardles, Nos. 8 and 3.

CONSTRUCTION OF THE FROME CUT-OFF, 1931.

At both Westbury and Frome, on the Great Western main line to the West of England, junctions and sharp curves enforced very severe speed restrictions. In 1930 the G.W.R. decided that two new short lengths of line should be constructed to bypass these places so speeding up considerably West of England expresses not scheduled to call at either Westbury or Frome.

The building of the two cut-offs were entrusted to the railway contracting firm of Logan and Hemingway, and work commenced in 1930. Amongst Logan and Hemingway's stud of locomotives were several 0-6-0 saddle-tanks built by Manning, Wardle and Company, and five of these most attractive engines were employed on the construction of the Westbury and Frome cut-offs.

93.　Logan and Hemingway's 0-6-0ST. No. 3, built by Manning, Wardle in 1888, maker's number 1069.

94.
Manning, Wardle 0-6-0 saddle-tanks Nos. 8 and 3, Both engines were absolutely immaculate, with gleaming brass and copper fittings and scrupulously clean paintwork.

All these pictures were taken on a Sunday when no work was in progress — and good luck played quite a part in how I obtained them. During the summer term we were allowed home for the week-end at half-term, and for weeks beforehand I would be planning how these two brief days of bliss should be spent. On the Sunday of the summer half-term in 1931, I asked my Father if he would take me for a ride in the car to the Frome area so that I could investigate a rumour I had heard that there was some new railway construction going on there. These pictures are the result of that successful "exploration".

95. Another of the Manning, Wardles sitting on top of a newly constructed embankment. Could this have been Logan and Hemingway's No. 10 which was also used on this contract? In 1935 the firm of Logan and Hemingway went into liquidation and No. 10 was sold to the Cranford Ironstone Company who named the engine "Sir Berkeley". In 1957 "Sir Berkeley" was overhauled and the brass-bound weatherboard was replaced by an open-backed cab. Shortly after this the engine was transferred to the Byfield Ironstone Quarries — see picture 257.

96. Logan and Hemingway's 0-6-0ST. No. 8 built by Manning, Wardle in 1888, maker's number 1079.

97. 30 years on . . . . 4th March, 1961.
"Castle" class No. 5058 "Earl of Clancarty", in charge of the down "Royal Duchy", passes the same spot — picture 92 — where I had photographed the two Manning Wardles in 1931.

98.

"King Arthur" class 4-6-0 No. 744, "Maid of Astolat", climbing towards Semley with the down "Atlantic Coast Express". No. 744 entered service in 1919 and was one of twenty N15 class engines designed by R.W. Urie for the London and South Western Railway. R.E.L. Maunsell, who succeeded Urie, based his "King Arthur" class engines on the Urie design, and the original twenty engines, modified to some extent, were incorporated into the "King Arthur" class, becoming known as "Urie Arthurs".

THE SOUTHERN RAILWAY, NEAR TISBURY

In the early 'thirties my eldest sister and her husband lived in a delightful house a little to the west of Tisbury in the heart of the Wiltshire countryside. Their home stood in the most beautiful surroundings on a hillside, and overlooked the Southern main line in the valley below as it climbed westwards from Tisbury towards Semley. As the Easter and summer holidays drew near, I would look forward eagerly to being invited down to stay for a few days.

99. An up local hauled by one of the Woolwich-built "N" class 2-6-0s. (See pictures 9 and 10). Parts for one hundred of these locomotives had been manufactured but only 50 locomotives were actually assembled and these were bought subsequently by the Southern Railway. See also pictures 108 and 118.

100.

One of Drummond's C8 class 4-4-0s, No. 297, passes by in charge of a down local. There were only ten engines in this class which came out in 1898 — one year before Drummond's much better known and highly successful T9s.

101.

"King Arthur" class 4-6-0 No. 746 "Pendragon" — another "Urie Arthur" — sweeps downhill towards Tisbury with an up express. One of the most noticeable external modifications carried out by Maunsell on these engines, was the replacement of the rather severe Urie chimney with one of his own handsome design.

102.

In the early 'thirties, "King Arthurs" had a virtual monopoly of all express trains west of Salisbury — which pleased me because I was very fond of these engines. This down express was hauled by one of Maunsell's "King Arthurs", No. 457 "Sir Bedivere", built at Eastleigh in 1925. It will be noticed that No. 457 was coupled to one of Drummond's old "watercart" tenders with inside bearings.

CAMBRIDGE.

After four years of unmitigated misery at my public school, I went up to Cambridge where the sudden change to an atmosphere of friendliness and freedom was almost overwhelming. My happiness at being "back in civilisation" knew no bounds.

The railway scene around Cambridge had a tremendous amount to offer; on my very first visit to the station I had seen engines from no less than four different pre-grouping companies — The Great Eastern, Great Northern, London and North Western, and the Midland. But I had not been at the University long before, from the railway angle, the worst occurred! — I got hopelessly hooked on motor racing. Although, as recounted in the introduction to this book, I never lost my love of trains, my railway photography virtually ceased from 1934 until after the Second World War.

103. Ex-Great Eastern "B.12" 4-6-0 No. 8512 waiting impatiently to set off with an up express for Liverpool Street. The fitting behind the chimney is an A.C.F.I. feed-water heater. "B.12"s that carried this device were often referred to as "Hikers", because of the resemblance to a walker carrying a rucksack on his back!

104. Ex-Great Eastern 2-4-0 No. 7434 noses up to one of H.A. Ivatt's Great Northern small-boilered Atlantics. These engines — the first Atlantics to appear in Britain — were designed in 1898, to be followed 4 years later by Ivatt's much better known large-boilered Atlantics. (See pictures 441 to 443.)

105.

No. 7388, one of Holden's outstanding class R24 0-6-0 tank engines designed for the Great Eastern Railway in 1890. In L.N.E.R. days these most useful little engines, of which no less than 230 had been built, became class J69.

106.

Ex-G.N.R. 0-6-0 No. 3539 passes by, light engine. This was an Ivatt design, although by the time the first of the class appeared in 1911, H.G. Ivatt had retired, and H.N. Gresley had become Locomotive Superintendent of the Great Northern Railway. In G.N.R. days the engines were known as the "536" class, but on the formation of the L.N.E.R. they became class J6.

107.

4-4-0 No. 8847, one of the very handsome ex-Great Eastern "Claud Hamilton" class engines. In 1922 a start had been made on re-building the "Claud Hamiltons" with larger boilers of 5ft. diameter. No. 8847 carries one of these boilers and it may be interesting to compare this view of her, with the "Claud Hamiltons" illustrated in pictures 24 and 25.

108. "Woolwich" class K1 2-6-0 No. 391 nearing Dublin with an up express in October, 1948. Reference has already been made (illustrations 9 and 99) to Woolwich Arsenal manufacturing parts for one hundred locomotives, but only erecting fifty. Twenty-seven sets of these parts were bought by Irish railways, twelve sets being acquired by the Midland Great Western Railway and fifteen more by the Great Southern Railways after the railways in the then Irish Free State had been amalgamated in 1925. (It appears however that only twenty-six engines were erected from the twenty-seven sets of parts). This transaction was the more interesting because the designer of these "Woolwich" 2-6-0s was R. E. L. Maunsell, who had been locomotive superintendent of the Great Southern and Western Railway in 1911-13,

PART 4
Ireland, 1948-51

One day shortly after the end of the war, I received a letter from the well-known Irish railway enthusiast and photographer, the late Mr. J. Macartney Robbins. He was coming over to England to see the Somerset and Dorset line and wondered whether I would be prepared to mark his map for him with some of the good photographic spots. I replied saying that I had a better idea — why didn't he come and stay with me when I would be able to give him a "Cook's Tour" of the northern half of the line, showing him all my favourite locations. We had a very happy 'S & D' weekend together, and later, when I was over in Ireland in October 1949, Mr. Macartney Robbins returned the compliment by taking me on a marvellous day's tour round Dublin's Running Sheds.

109.

On a fresh morning in October 1948 "Tailte", one of E. C. Bredin's magnificent B1a class 4-6-0s, makes a regal departure from Kingsbridge Station, Dublin, with an express for Cork.

INCHICORE.

The Works and Dublin Running Shed of the Great Southern and Western Railway were situated at Inchicore. In 1925 the G.S. & W.R. lost its individuality when the railways lying wholly in the then Irish Free State were amalgamated to form the Great Southern Railways. In 1945 the G.S.R. in turn became part of Coras Iompair Eireann (The Transport Company of Ireland) and Inchicore is now the Works and Dublin Running Shed of C.I.E.

110. A year later, in October, 1949, I saw "Tailte" again. This time — temporarily minus her smokebox door — she was standing outside Inchicore Running Sheds alongside an elderly 4-4-0, No. 98 of class D17. "Tailte" and her two sisters, "Maedhbh" and "Macha", entered service in 1939-40; the 4-4-0, designed by J.A.F. Aspinall for the G.S. & W.R., was built in 1887.

111. To be broken up, or repaired? — a dejected line-up of locomotives await their fate outside Inchicore Works in October, 1949. Leading the group is ex-G.S. & W.R. D17 class 4-4-0 No. 11. Next comes an ex-M. G.W.R. J18 class 0-6-0, then an ex-M.G.W.R. J5 class 0-6-0, and bringing up the rear, an ex-D. & S.E.R. C3 class 4-4-2T.

112. K1 class 2-6-0 No. 384, B1a class 4-6-0 No. 802 "Tailte" and D17 class 4-4-0 No. 98.

INCHICORE

RUNNING SHED,

October 1949.

113. Ex-G.S. & W.R. class K3 2-6-0 No. 356, fitted experimentally with self-emptying smokebox tubes. These engines, designed by R. Coey in 1903, started off life as 0-6-0s, but for weight reasons were soon converted to 2-6-0s.

114. Four engines lined up outside the running shed – ex-G.S. & W.R. class K3 2-6-0 No. 356, class J15 0-6-0 No. 109, class D3 4-4-0 No. 332, and ex-G.S.R. class J15b 0-6-0 No. 712.

115. D15 class 4-4-0 No. 296, designed by J.G. Robinson (later of Great Central Railway fame) and built in 1896 for the Waterford, Limerick and Western Railway. Behind her stands D7 class 4-4-0 No. 538, designed by E. Cusack in 1909 for the Midland Great Western Railway.

116. D2 class 4-4-0 No. 323 designed by R. Coey for the Great Southern and Western Railway in 1904.

117.

In October 1949 the Inchicore shed pilot was this delightful 0-4-2 saddletank "Sambo", built in 1913 for the G.S. & W.R. to the design of R.E.L. Maunsell.

118.

Standing in the sunshine outside Broadstone shed in October, 1949 — K1 class 2-6-0 No. 381 (another of the engines erected in Ireland from "Woolwich" parts) and 0-6-0T. No. 614, one of the J10 class designed by M. Atock for the Midland Great Western Railway in 1881.

BROADSTONE RUNNING SHED, DUBLIN.
October, 1949.

This was originally the Dublin motive power depot of the old Midland Great Western Railway.

119.

Standing on the turntable at Broadstone Shed is D5 class 4-4-0 No. 546. These engines were designed for the MGWR by E. Cusack in 1902.

120.

Another of E. Cusack's designs for the M. G.W.R., D7 class 4-4-0 No. 539 draws forward past the shed with some wagons. The first of these engines came out in 1909.

121. In 1948 the G.N.R. (I) had put into service five splendid new three-cylinder 4-4-0s designed by H.R. McIntosh. When Mr. Macartney Robbins took me to Amiens Street shed in 1949, I had the good fortune to see one of these VS class 4-4-0s, No. 208 "Lagan".

AMIENS STREET RUNNING SHED, DUBLIN.
October, 1949

These were the Dublin running sheds of the Great Northern Railway (Ireland) which linked Belfast, in Northern Ireland, with Dublin in the Republic of Ireland.

122. G.N.R. (I) S class 4-4-0 No. 173 "Galtee More", designed by C. Clifford in 1913.

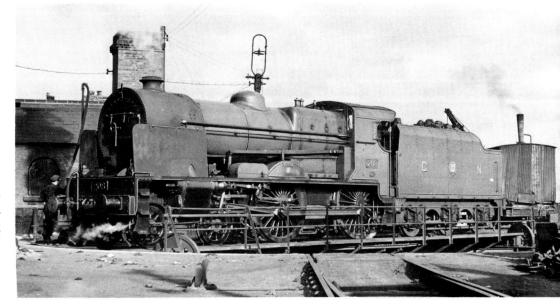

123. "Lagan", just one year old, and with her beautiful blue livery sparkling in the sunshine, looked really superb as she posed on the turn-table.

SKIBBEREEN. July, 1950.

Whilst on holiday in south west Ireland in the summer of 1950, someone told me that they thought the Baltimore branch was still being
worked by an old Ivatt 2-4-2 tank. So on one of our "day expeditions"
we decided to look in at Skibbereen, on the Baltimore branch, to find
out. We found the Ivatt all right, but also far more than this! The
branch line train was not due for over half an hour, but as we drew near
to Skibbereen I was surprised to see a column of steam rising into the
still summer air from the station yard — and there, to my intense
excitement we found one of the narrow gauge Schull and Skibbereen
Light Railway engines in steam and in the act of pulling out from their
shed the other two engines! The Schull and Skibbereen Light Railway
had been closed for some years, but it turned out that Mr. Cyril Fry —
an eminent Irish railway enthusiast — had arranged for the stock to be
pulled out for him to measure for modelling purposes.*

124. STANDARD GAUGE — Class F6
2-4-2T. No. 33, designed by H.A.
Ivatt for the Great Southern and
Western Railway in 1892, sets off
for Drimoleague with the afternoon mixed train.

125. NARROW GAUGE — 0-4-4T. No. 6s, built
by T. Green & Son in 1893, pulls out the
other two Schull and Skibbereen engines,
4-4-0 tanks No. 4s built by Naysmith,
Wilson in 1888 and No. 3s "Kent", built by
Peckett & Sons in 1914. No. 6s started her
life on the Cork and Muskerry Light Railway,
but after this line had closed, she was transferred, in 1938, to the S. & S.L.R.

*Several pictures of this day's "event" appear in my book "The Narrow Gauge Charm of Yesterday", published by the Oxford Publishing
Company.*

KENMARE.

In 1951 I returned again to Kerry in South West Ireland for my summer holiday, staying at Parknasilla, some 12 miles west of Kenmare. Kenmare was the terminus of a branch line from Headford Junction, and in the summer of 1951 there were two trains a day, often of mixed stock and hauled by either an elderly 4-4-0 or 0-6-0.

126. D19 class 4-4-0 No. 13 standing in Kenmare station with the 1.15p.m. mixed train for Headford Junction on 25th June, 1951. The day before, No. 13's right hand spectacle glass had come off second best in an encounter with a firing iron, and the window was patched temporarily with a piece of wood.

127. The previous summer, on 30th June, 1950, I had taken this picture of J15 class 0-6-0 No. 182 arriving at Kenmare with the 3.40 p.m. from Headford Junction.

128. D19 class 4-4-0 No. 7 standing on the turntable at Kenmare.

KENMARE
June, 1951.

129. The cab-side number plate of D19 class 4-4-0 No. 13. These engines, designed by A. MacDonnell for the Great Southern and Western Railway, were built between 1877 and 1880. As the plate indicates, No. 13 was rebuilt at Inchicore in 1900.

130. The cab of D19 class No. 13.

131. No. 13 resting in the station yard. After the morning train from Headford Junction had arrived at Kenmare at 12.10 p.m., the engine would first of all be turned and then have her tender replenished. Following this, she would pull out from the platform her two coaches, plus any wagons that had been attached to the train, and remove them to the station yard — where they would sit until it was time to reverse back into the platform for the departure at 1.15p.m.

132.

No. 13 sets off from Kenmare at 1.15p.m. with her mixed train for the run back to Headford Junction.

133.

D19 class 4-4-0 No. 7 standing alongside a C4 class 4-4-2T.

134.

J15 class 0-6-0 No. 127. These outstanding and most useful engines, designed by A. Mac-Donnell for the G.S. & W.R., first appeared in 1866, and batches continued to be built up to 1903, when the class numbered one hundred and eleven engines.

135.

D19 class No. 7, another of A. MacDonnell's excellent designs for the G.S. & W.R. Built in 1877–80, they were the first 4-4-0 engines in Ireland.

THE TRALEE SHED OF THE 3ft. GAUGE TRALEE AND DINGLE LIGHT RAILWAY

136. Inside the shed, October, 1949.

2-6-0T. No. 8T., built by the Hunslet Engine Company in 1910. Just visible behind her is the cab of No. 5T. also built by Hunslet, and the only 2-6-2T. on the line.

137. Outside the shed, July, 1950.

Two of the Hunslet built 2-6-0 tank engines, No. 8T. (1910) and No. 1T. (1889).

THE TRALEE AND DINGLE LIGHT RAILWAY.

From Tralee in County Kerry, this delightful 3ft. gauge line ran south west for 31 miles through the magnificent, wild beauty of the Dingle peninsula. Since 1947 there had been only one train a month, a cattle special run in connection with Dingle Fair, but this was a hopelessly uneconomic situation, and the line finally closed in 1953.

On the last Friday in June, 1951 — a glorious summer's day — I followed the train for the whole of her journey from Tralee to Dingle, taking many pictures on the way.*

138. From the terminus of the narrow gauge Tralee and Dingle Light Railway, a line ran through the streets to some exchange sidings in the standard gauge goods yard. On the footplate of No. 8T., proceeding cautiously along the street, is the late Mr. Cyril Fry.

139. Friday, 29th June, 1951. Nos, 1T. and 2T., with their train of empty cattle wagons, have covered some nine miles on their journey to Dingle and are drawing near to Castlegregory Junction.

*A large number of these pictures appear in my book "The Narrow Gauge Charm of Yesterday", published by the Oxford Publishing Company.

140. In the course of the journey to Dingle, the line climbed to 684 feet above sea level to cross the Slieve Mish mountain range. In this picture Nos. 1T. and 2T. have just commenced the extremely severe 4-mile climb, much of it at 1 in 30, up to the Glenmore Pass.

41. With just a few hundred yards to go to Glenagalt bridge, Nos. 1T. and 2T. are nearing the summit and the end of the 4-mile climb. This was *very* nearly a picture of tragedy — my sister stood rooted to the spot as a sheep, squeezing through the fence, escaped death by a hair's breadth!

PART 5

Favourite Lines

THE SOMERSET AND DORSET.

Ever since I was a small boy, my favourite railway has always been the Somerset and Dorset. I think it was probably the beautiful blue colour in which the engines and coaches were painted which attracted me in the first place — to see a royal blue Somerset and Dorset train running through the fresh green countryside on a fine spring morning was a magnificent and unforgettable sight.

But it wasn't long before I came to realise that the Somerset and Dorset was far more than just a pretty blue train. For the railway enthusiast, the S & D had just about everything one could wish for — a wide variety of engines, including the incomparable S & D class 7F 2-8-0s; beautiful scenery; long, steep gradients necessitating engines having to work very hard; and a most friendly, warm-hearted and close-knit staff.

As I have already devoted a whole book* to the Somerset and Dorset, these are just four token pages to a wonderful line which has so many happy memories for me. Actually there are two more pages on the Somerset and Dorset further on — I couldn't resist the temptation of bringing it in again under the section on branch lines.

142. *The family spirit . . . .*
The staff on the Somerset and Dorset were like one big family — they all seemed to know one another. On Sunday, 8th November, 1959, S & D 7F 2-8-0 No. 53802, in charge of an engineer's train, had a lengthy wait at Midford — so what was more natural than that the train crew and the signalman should get together for a general chat. From the left — signalman Harry Wiltshire, driver Harry Starkey, guard William Parratt and fireman Harry Shearn.

143. *Beautiful scenery . . . .*

On a spring afternoon in 1954 the down "Pines Express", hauled by 2P 4-4-0 No. 40634 (built for the S & D in 1928) and S.R. Pacific No. 34040 "Crewkerne", has just emerged from the mile-long Combe Down tunnel and is running downhill over Tucking Mill viaduct towards Midford.

"The Somerset and Dorset — an English Cross-Country Railway", published by the Oxford Publishing Company.

Variety in motive power . . . .

A contrast in engines used over the Somerset and Dorset.

144.   9F 2-10-0 No. 92203, being driven with verve by Peter Smith, sweeps through the curves south west of Wellow with the 7.35 a.m. (SO) Nottingham to Bournemouth on an overcast day in July, 1960. At the time, No. 92203 was only just over one year old, having entered service in April, 1959. Happily, this 9F is still 'alive', having been purchased by the famous artist, David Shepherd. No. 92203, now named "Black Prince", is kept on the East Somerset Railway at Cranmore, where visitors are welcome.

145.   For many decades the ex-Midland Johnson 1P 0-4-4 tanks gave excellent service over the Somerset and Dorset. In this picture, No. 58072, built for the Midland Railway by Neilson & Company in 1893, is arriving at Midsomer Norton with the 6.05 p.m. down local from Bath to Binegar on 26th April, 1955.

THE SOMERSET AND DORSET

146. *Long steep gradients. . . .*

Maximum effort − 1 in 50 up and sixteen on!
Ex-Midland 2P 4-4-0 No. 40527 and S & D 7F 2-8-0
No. 53808, in charge of a pigeon special, have just
emerged from the quarter-mile-long, narrow bore and
unventilated Devonshire tunnel, in their struggle up
the 1 in 50 bank out of Bath on a miserable day in
August, 1955.

147. *The incomparable S & D 7F 2-8-0s. . . .*

No. 53807 hurries by with an evening freight in the summer of 1964. These excellent engines were designed by Sir Henry Fowler specially for the Somerset and Dorset. Six were built at the Derby Works of the Midland Railway in 1914 and these proved so successful that a further five were constructed in 1925 by Robert Stephenson and Company of Darlington. As a class, they gave outstanding service to the Somerset and Dorset for fifty years, the last one, No. 53807, not being withdrawn until September, 1964.

Happily two S&D 7Fs still exist. No. 53808 has been preserved by the Somerset and Dorset Circle: and No. 53809 is being completely reconditioned for use on the North Yorkshire Moors Line.

148.
Reverse curves and single-line sections – two more interesting features of the Somerset and Dorset . . . .

Between Midford and Radstock the Somerset and Dorset abounded in reverse curves, the line twisting and turning as it followed closely the contours of the Midford and Wellow valleys.

On Saturday, 10th August, 1957, S.R. Pacific No. 34107 "Blandford Forum", assisted by 4F. 0-6-0 No. 44146 is heading south from Midford with the 9.10 a.m. (SO) Birmingham to Bournemouth. On the up line, 2P 4-4-0 No. 40698 and S.R. Pacific No. 34043 "Combe Martin", in charge of the 9.55 (SO) Bournemouth to Leeds, have been held at Midford's up outer home signal, waiting their turn for the single-line section into Bath.

FAVOURITE LINES
Grayrigg to Tebay.

In the days when the Somerset and Dorset was a busy, thriving railway, it became almost a habit for me to spend most Saturdays somewhere on the line. But in 1958 the Western Region of British Railways gained a dominating control over the Somerset and Dorset and it was not long before certain ominous changes began to take place. Goods traffic started to be diverted away from the line and when at the end of the 1962 summer service, the "Pines Express" and all other through trains were re-routed away from the Somerset and Dorset, the ultimate intention of the Western Region to close the line could no longer be concealed. The once happy atmosphere amongst the S & D staff changed to a mood of dejection and bitterness, not just because their line was to be closed, but for the manner in which this was being brought about.

So in the early 'sixties I started to turn away from the sad scene on the Somerset and Dorset, and commenced looking at other lines. For many years my friend Derek Cross had been trying to persuade me to visit Shap, but loath to leave my beloved S & D, I had made one excuse after another for not making the long journey north from Somerset. However, in 1965, with the Somerset and Dorset nearing the end, off I went to Westmorland; and there, it was not the famous Shap incline that drew me, but the line just to the south. After the Somerset and Dorset, no stretch of railway brought me greater pleasure than the seven miles of the old L.N.W.R. main line from Grayrigg through the Lune Gorge to Tebay. I was entranced by the quiet, remote beauty of the Westmorland fells — no madding crowds, just utter peace and serenity, broken only by the lonely cry of a curlew or the distant bleating of a sheep. Oh what happy days those were! But never again, for all that was yesterday. Today we have Progress — with the railway electrified and the six-lane M6 motorway carving a vast concrete swath through the Lune Gorge.

149. GRAYRIGG. One location which attracted me greatly was at the western end of Grayrigg where a small over-bridge crossed the line. I was enchanted by the scene from this spot, particularly on fine evenings when the distant fells stood out clear-cut in the background. Evening after evening I would end my day's photography standing on this small bridge at the western end of Grayrigg, but the sad fact is that the appearance of a southbound steam-hauled train, very rarely coincided with the sun being out. The same could not be said for diesels, however, and I have one sequence of 16 mm. colour film taken in dramatic evening lighting of a diesel-hauled express. Whenever I look at this piece of film I think how marvellous it must be to be a great artist like Terence Cuneo or David Shepherd who, with a wave of the wand — or rather, the paintbrush — would transform the diesel-hauled express of the 1960s into a 1924 train of L.N.W.R. "plum and spilt-milk" coaches hauled by a "Claughton", just re-painted in L.M.S. red.

However — back to reality. In the early evening, and with the sun not really quite far enough round, a Stanier "Black Five", No. 45105, passes by with a south-bound goods. (See also picture 475.)

150. MORNING — "Britannia" Pacific No. 70050 comes majestically through the cutting east of Grayrigg Box in charge of a down goods on a lovely spring morning in 1965.

GRAYRIGG.

151. EVENING — a sullen day of drenching rain in April 1967, had matured into a vivid, fragrant late spring evening, as "Britannia" Pacific No. 70005 topped Grayrigg bank with a north-bound freight. In the rear, 2-6-4T. No. 42210 was about to drop off after giving banking assistance up from Oxenholme.

GRAYRIGG.

152. On an overcast day in April 1965 Stanier class 5 No. 44672, working very hard, passes Grayrigg Box with a heavy parcels train which she had brought up from Oxenholme unassisted.

153. When north-bound parcels trains required a banker, the usual practice was for one of the Oxenholme 2-6-4 tanks to couple ahead of the train engine and assist the whole way up to Shap summit. On 16th July, 1966, Stanier class 5 No. 45109 and her assistant 2-6-4T. No. 42210, were making light work of their north-bound parcels as they topped Grayrigg bank.

154. A sunny morning in July 1966. 9F 2-10-0 No. 92019, in charge of an oil train, has been diverted into the down loop to get out of the way of "Britannia" Pacific No. 70025, going extremely well with a north-bound parcels train.

155. On a very hot, hazy day in August 1967, one of the interesting ex-Crosti 9F 2-10-0s, No. 92021, hauling a south-bound freight, makes a cautious approach to Grayrigg, where she was about to be "tucked away" in the up loop to allow an express to overtake her.

156. "Britannia" Pacific No. 70018 passes by with a south-bound freight. In the foreground is the branch that diverged from the main line at Lowgill to run down the Lune valley through Sedbergh to Ingleton and the "other" Clapham Junction.

157. After the Ingleton line had been closed in 1964, it was used for the dumping of spent ballast. On 29th July, 1965, Ivatt 2-6-0 No. 43017 had been down to Sedbergh to collect some empty ballast wagons and is seen here coming back over Beck Foot viaduct towards Lowgill with her train.

158. On 14th April 1966, "Britannia" Pacific No. 70023 sauntered past, in no apparent hurry, with an up parcels train.

159. 7 a.m. on a crisp autumn morning. Stanier class 5 No. 44832 running south with a goods, and leaving behind her a long trail of white exhaust in the still, early morning air.

NORTH OF LOWGILL.

160. I shall always remember the amusing prelude to the taking of this picture. My friend Norman Lockett was with me and we were on our way from Lowgill to the Lune Gorge. We had been walking – with permits, I hasten to add – for about a mile and were approaching the spot where the line turned north, when suddenly both of us saw it at the same moment – smoke rising above the bluff in the hillside round which the line curved. Ciné camera, tripod, picnic lunches etc. were hurriedly deposited on the ground and a mad scramble made up the side of the cutting to photograph the approaching train. Our rather breathless anticipation, however, was short-lived, for we soon realised that the smoke was not moving; it was, in fact, coming from a bonfire just lit by some gangers round the corner. Rather sheepishly we climbed down the side of the cutting, gathered up our scattered equipment and started walking again, but we hadn't taken more than a few paces when a high-pitched singing noise from the continuous welded rail really *did* herald the approach of a train. Another unceremonious dumping of ciné camera etc., and scramble up the bank ensued, to be rewarded this time by "Britannia" Pacific No. 70013 appearing round the corner with this long train of empty wagons.

One of the bank engines, 2-6-4T. No. 42251, passes by, light engine, on her way from Tebay down to Oxenholme.

161.   Stanier class 5 No. 45048 and "Britannia" Pacific No. 70031, double-heading a heavy parcels train, draw near to the Lune Gorge one afternoon in late spring, 1967.

162.   Stanier class 5 No. 44964 leaves the Lune Gorge behind as she heads south towards Lowgill with an up goods in the early autumn of 1966.

163. 9F 2-10-0 No. 92056 running north with a banana train. Both this picture, and the one below, were taken in the Lune Gorge on 17th April, 1967 — an absolutely perfect day. Nothing disturbed the peace on this warm spring afternoon, except for the occasional cry of a curlew or the distant barking of a dog rounding up sheep on the far side of the gorge.

THE LUNE GORGE.

164. "Britannia" Pacific No. 70032 drifts leisurely through the Lune Gorge with a train of pipes.

65. At the southern end of Dillicar troughs the ground used to rise sharply on the west side to form a ready-made grandstand, and it was here, amidst clusters of foxgloves, that I settled down one perfect afternoon in July 1966 to watch the trains. The hot sun and the intermittent droning of bees exploring the foxgloves had a soporific effect on me, and I nearly missed this shot of Stanier class 5 No. 44986 running south over the troughs with an up freight! Today my "grandstand" no longer exists — it was levelled and buried under masses of concrete for the M6 motorway.

TEBAY — DILLICAR TROUGHS.

166.

9F 2-10-0 No. 92019 takes water as she passes over the troughs in charge of an up freight one morning in early July 1966.

168. These bas-reliefs of Great Western broad gauge engines are on the wall of the office block facing the main line. They are readily visible from passing trains, but I wonder how many passengers notice them?

PART 6

Swindon

Just the one word SWINDON always had a slightly magical ring about it for me. These famous Works, built by the broad gauge Great Western Railway in 1841/2 were the birthplace of G.W.R. engines for over a century.

The Great Western Railway, and their successors the Western Region of British Railways, used to welcome week-end visits to Swindon Works when organised parties would be shown round by official guides. Together with fellow members of the Bath Railway Society, I paid several happy and interesting visits to Swindon in the 1950s.

167. "Chimneys and bas-reliefs".

169.

Swindon visit, November, 1959. Three of my friends in the Bath Railway Society, Ken Padfield, Ron Hurst and Norman Lockett, pose in front of No. 7029 "Clun Castle" with — centre — Mr. Stratford, the chief guide and, on the right holding the Works cat, Mr. Cooper, assistant guide.

170.

Another nostalgic link with the past — the weathercock which adorns the Mechanics' Institute opposite the Works entrance, is a silhouette of the broad gauge engine "Lord of the Isles".

171. For many years the Great Western preserved two of their most famous broad gauge engines, "North Star", one of their very earliest engines built by Robert Stephenson & Co. in 1837, and the magnificent 4-2-2 "Lord of the Isles". Then in 1906, suddenly and inexplicably, the order went forth that both were to be broken up.

It seems that later the Great Western must have regretted destroying these two heirlooms, for in 1925 they went to the trouble of making a replica of "North Star" to take part in the Railway Centenary celebrations. Afterwards for many years this replica stood on a high pedestal in "A" shop, until transferred to Swindon Railway Museum where it may now be inspected.

A CONTRAST IN FOOTPLATES.

172.

The "North Star" (replica) 1837.

173.

— and a Hawksworth "County" class 4-6-0 of 1945.

174.
2-8-0 No. 4700 standing between some "Castle" class driving wheels and a reconditioned "Castle" boiler. On the floor in the foreground are some completed eccentric straps.

175.
Amongst the engines undergoing overhaul in "A" shop in April, 1956, were ex-R.O.D. 2-8-0 No. 3015, "Castle" class 4-6-0 No. 5081 "Lockheed Hudson", and a "Hall" class 4-6-0.

176.
Fifty-three of the B.R. standard 9F 2-10-0s were built at Swindon; on 27th September, 1959, No. 92213 was nearing completion in "A" shop. This splendid giant was to have a life of only seven years, for when still in her prime, she was withdrawn in October, 1966, made redundant by dieselisation.

"A" ERECTING SHOP.

177. No. 4700, the first of Churchward's mixed traffic 2-8-0s with 5ft. 8in. coupled wheels, was built at Swindon in 1919. On 8th November, 1959, she was standing in "A" shop, her overhaul completed, looking an absolute picture in fully lined-out green livery — something with which she was never adorned in Great Western days.

178.

In 1904 G.W.R. 4-4-0 "City of Truro" achieved fame when Mr. Charles Rous-Marten, timing a special mail train that she was hauling, assessed that the engine had reached a speed of 102.3 m.p.h. down Wellington bank. After her withdrawal from service in 1931, the 4-4-0 was preserved in York Railway Museum. In 1957 "City of Truro" was brought out from retirement and given a complete overhaul at Swindon prior to being used for hauling special trains. In April, 1958, she was in "A" shop for minor attention and "touching-up" before hauling the first of the season's special trains. (See pictures 210, 211, 432, 433 and 445.)

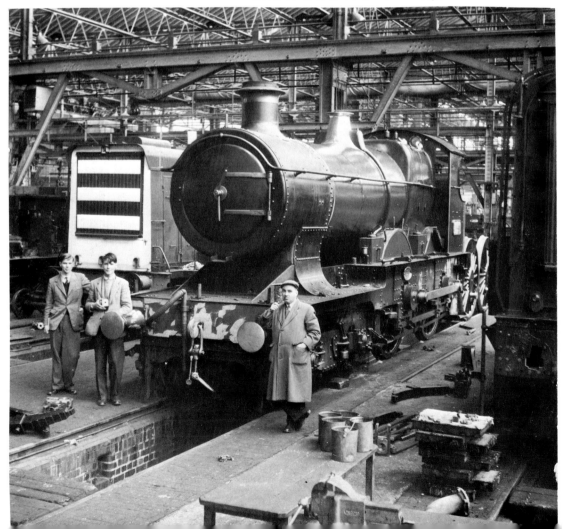

179. Engines standing outside the Works in April, 1958, awaiting attention. In the line-up are — 2-6-2T. No. 3190, ex-R.O.D. 2-8-0 No. 3041, 4-6-0s No. 5034 "Corfe Castle", No. 1002 "County of Berks" and No. 7034 "Ince Castle".

"BEFORE".

Engines waiting to be moved into the Works for overhaul.

180. Ex-R.O.D. 2-8-0 No. 3041. After the First World War the Great Western took over some of the Robinson-designed Great Central 2-8-0s which had been built in large numbers for use by the Railway Operating Division of the Army. As the years went by, the Great Western's engines acquired quite a few "Swindon" features. No. 3041 has a 47XX class chimney and a typical G.W.R. safety-valve bonnet.

181.

B.R. standard class 2 MT 2-6-0 No. 78005 and ex G.W.R. "Hall" class 4-6-0 No 6904 "Charfield Hall" standing outside "A" shop in April 1956. The presence of No 78005 awaiting entry into the Works surprised me, for she was less than three years old

.. and "AFTER"...

ngines standing outside in im-
aculate condition.

182. The overhaul of locomotives was carried out in "A" shop. Tenders were dealt with in a shop of their own and in this picture, taken in September, 1959, five freshly overhauled engines are standing outside this shop, waiting to be reunited with tenders. The engines are four 4-6-0s, No. 6915 "Mursley Hall", No. 4963 "Rignall Hall, No. 6935 "Browsholme Hall" and No. 7901 "Dodington Hall" — and sandwiched in the middle, 28XX class 2-8-0 No. 3823.

183.

4-6-0 No. 7034 "Ince Castle" in November, 1959. It will be observed that since the picture taken of her in April, 1958 (opposite page, top) she had acquired a double chimney.

184.

Just overhauled, and immaculate in a fresh coat of black paint, 2-6-0 No. 9309 stands outside "A" shop in April, 1956.

185.

Still retaining the wedge-shaped cab front from the G.W.R.'s brief dally with stream-lining in the mid-'thirties, No. 6014 "King Henry VII" gleams in the autumn sunshine outside the works on 27th September, 1959.

ENGINE VARIETY.

One of the attractions about a visit to Swindon was the variety of engines one would see. On visits organised by the Bath Railway Society, we used to travel up by rail, and as our train ran past the Works everyone would look out eagerly to see what engines were "on view" outside "A" shop.

186. The "Kings" were the largest and most powerful engines built by the Great Western. No. 6000 "King George V", complete with the bell presented to her when she went to America in 1927, is standing outside the weigh-house in November, 1959. In the background on the right is "Castle" class 4-6-0 No. 5063 "Earl Baldwin".

187. Six small tank engines clustered together outside the office block in August, 1960.

Engines from Welsh railways which had been incorporated into the Great Western when the railways of Britain were amalgamated in 1923.

188. Ex-Rhymney Railway 0-6-2T. No. 35, built in 1921 (note acquisition of "Swindon" safety valve bonnet) and Hawksworth 0-6-0 pannier tank No. 9451, built at Swindon after the G.W.R. had been nationalised.

189. Two ex-Taff Vale Railway 0-6-2 tanks Nos. 351 and 388. Both had been rebuilt by the G.W.R. which accounts for the several "Swindon" features.

190. Swindon had the sad honour of building British Railway's last steam locomotive, 9F 2-10-0 No. 92220. The engine was completed in March 1960 and to commemorate the occasion she was given a copper-capped chimney and painted in lined-out green livery. On Friday, 18th March, there was a ceremony in "A" shop at Swindon when No. 92220 was named "Evening Star". This picture was taken after the official proceedings were over. Standing on the right (wearing hat) is Mr. R.H.N. Bryant, Chief staff and administrative assistant to the C.M. & E.E., Western Region, and with him is Mr. A. Simpkins, chief foreman, erecting shop.

191. On Friday, 18th March, 1960, as part of the ceremony for naming "Evening Star", two famous old engines had been on exhibition inside "A" shop – the Caledonian Railway 4-2-2 No. 123 and the Great Western's 4-4-0 "City of Truro". This picture was taken on the following Sunday morning as a rather grubby pannier tank was in the process of moving the old engines from the Works to the stock shed.

THE END OF AN ERA.

192. In 1965 steam traction on the Western Region was drawing to a close, and on 11th April I paid my last visit to Swindon. British Railways had sold 4-6-0 No. 4079 "Pendennis Castle" to a private buyer, and the Works had made a splendid job of overhauling the engine and re-painting her in Great Western livery. This picture was taken after a brief ceremony when the engine had been handed over to her new owner. (See also picture 455.)

193. Later in 1960 I again saw "City of Truro" at Swindon. On this occasion, 9th August, she was standing in the down platform of the station at the head of a local train for Bristol. Today, "City of Truro" is in Swindon Railway Museum — and the down platform and buildings no longer exist, having been demolished when the station was modernised.

PART 7
Engine Testing

A locomotive on test always interested me greatly. There was no problem in knowing when and where to see a new engine — or one that had just been overhauled — on test, since for years the Great Western, and later the Western Region, had used the same local services between Swindon and Bristol as "running-in" turns. But information on engines engaged in a Controlled Road Test, was a different matter altogether. "Security" seemed very tight about these runs, and normally the first I would know about any such event was on being greeted by a railwayman with the remark "You should have been here yesterday!" However, just now and again the proverbial "little bird" did whisper in my ear.

194. In July, 1953, No. 6001 "King Edward VII", after being modified at Swindon, and fitted temporarily with an indicator shelter, was engaged in some most interesting Controlled Road Tests between Reading and Stoke Gifford. Standing in front of the engine in Stoke Gifford yard on 2nd July are (left) Mr. O.S. Nock, the well-known railway author, and Mr. S.O. Ell, Assistant Engineer Locomotive Testing, Swindon.

For this run, No. 6001 had a trailing load of the dynamometer car and twenty-four coaches — 795 tons!

195. One reason for the Reading to Stoke Gifford route being used for these Controlled Road Tests, was that there were triangle junctions at both ends, so simplifying the turning of the engine and dynamometer car. In this picture, No. 6001 plus the dynamometer car and one coach (which carried weighed bags of coal) are in the process of turning at Filton Junction.

196.

Three weeks later, on 23rd July, 1953, No. 6001 carried out another Controlled Road Test, burning lower grade coal. She is seen here, with a trailing load of the dynamometer car and twenty-two coaches, climbing towards Sodbury tunnel on the return run to Reading.

Ex-Great Western Hawksworth "County" class 4-6-0s engaged in Controlled Road Tests. During the test programme, the engines were fitted temporarily with indicator shelters.

197. On 19th January, 1954, No. 1000 "County of Middlesex" draws near to Stoke Gifford with a test train of thirteen coaches and the dynamometer car. At this date No. 1000 still had her original handsome double chimney.

198.

Later in the year, No. 1009. "County of Carmarthen", after she had been modified at Swindon, ran a Controlled Road Test on 16th November, with a trailing load of twenty-one coaches plus the dynamometer car. In this picture of No. 1009 approaching Stoke Gifford note the ugly stovepipe chimney with which she had been fitted.

RUNNING-IN TURNS
— NEW ENGINES.

199. B.R. "Britannia" Pacifics were built at Crewe, the first one emerging from the works in January, 1951. Nos. 70017 to 70029 were allocated to the Western Region and in July, 1951, No. 70017 "Arrow" arrived at Swindon for fitting with G.W.R. automatic train control apparatus. Early in August No. 70017 appeared at Bath on one of the regular "running-in" turns, the 10.05 a.m. Bristol — Swindon local.

Whenever possible, I used to try and get to Bath station on Saturday mornings to see this train which arrived at 10.30 a.m., and then set back into the middle road, where it would stand for the next thirty minutes. As it was rare for the same engine to remain on this "running-in" turn for more than two days, every Saturday would produce a different engine — and invariably in immaculate condition. For what more could one have asked? — and all this pleasure for the price of a platform ticket!

200. Brand new, and just ex-Works, No. 7018 "Drysllwyn Castle" sets off from Saltford station with the 5.00 p.m. down local from Swindon to Bristol on 26th May, 1949. On fine summer evenings I would often go over to Saltford to see this train, for it was a regular "running-in" turn and would invariably produce an interesting engine. The Great Western "Castle" class had first appeared in 1923, and so good was the design that in 1950 — twenty-seven years later, and three years after the G.W.R. had been nationalised — "Castles" were still being built at Swindon.

1. On 22nd June, 1949, the up morning "running-in" turn produced the famous engine No. 6000, "King George V", just re-painted in the new blue livery then being tried out by B.R. on the largest passenger engines.

RUNNING-IN TURNS
— ENGINES EX-WORKS AFTER OVERHAUL

202.

One of Churchward's "Star" class engines, No. 4058, "Princess Augusta", which had been fitted with outside elbow steam pipes, sitting in the middle road at Bath station on 6th June, 1949. She had also acquired one of Hawksworth's new straight-sided tenders — an unusual pairing for a "Star".

03.

vening "running-in" turn. hurchward mixed traffic -8-0 No. 4708 sets off rom Saltford on 29th May, 1956. She was ainted in unlined black – see picture 177.

204.
"Saint" class No. 2934 "Butleigh Court", 27th May, 1950.

RUNNING-IN TURNS AT BATH —

205.
"Hall" class No. 5958 "Knolton Hall", 28th March, 1959.

206.
"Grange" class No. 6818 "Hardwick Grange", 4th April, 1959.

4-CYLINDER TYPES

207.

"Star" class No. 4062 "Malmesbury Abbey", 15th May, 1954.

SIX VARIETIES OF GREAT WESTERN 4-6-0s.

208.

"Castle" class No. 7014 "Caerhays Castle", 28th February, 1959.

The 'Black Box' on the side of the smokebox contained a supply of oil for the Davies and Metcalfe patent valveless lubricator with which No. 7014 had been experimentally fitted. The lubricator can be seen mounted on the running plate ahead of the outside steam pipe.

209.

"King" class No. 6023 "King Edward II", 7th August, 1950.

Ex-G.W.R. 4-4-0, "CITY OF TRURO".

In 1956 something most exciting happened concerning the ex-Great Western 4-4-0 "City of Truro" — it was decided to bring this famous engine out from York Railway Museum, where she had been in retirement for many years, and put her back into traffic for hauling special trains. "City of Truro" was sent to Swindon for a thorough overhaul, and when the engine emerged in March, 1957, restored in her old livery, she looked absolutely superb. These two pictures were taken of "City of Truro" on 25th March, 1957, running-in after her overhaul. "City of Truro" also appears in pictures 178, 191, 193, 432, 433 and 445.

210. No. 3440 "City of Truro" standing in the middle road at Bath on 25th March, 1957.

211. Coasting into Bathampton station.

'KINGS' AND 'CASTLES' AT BATH.

212. No. 6007, "King William III", was standing in Bath station on the up "running-in" turn on 14th January, 1950, when No. 5035, "Coity Castle", arrived with the 9.05a.m. down express from Paddington.

213.

On 30th April, 1954, I was standing on the end of the up platform at Bath, waiting to photograph No. 6003 "King George IV", which was making a test run to assess the practicability of speeding up the "Bristolian". Just as the "King" — with the dynamometer car next to the engine — appeared in sight, No. 7036 "Ogmore Castle", which had been standing in the platform behind me, started to get under way with an up express. I just managed to get my picture — but it was a jolly close thing!

A 9F 2–10–0
ON TEST

214. 9F No. 92178 approaching Stoke Gifford on the misty morning of 29th January, 1958. The trailing load this day was fourteen bogies, including the dynamometer car.

During the 1950s, Swindon had done a lot of work on the 'front-end' of ex-Great Western 4-6-0s with a view to improving the draughting. In 1957 a further series of standard 9F 2-10-0s were being built at Swindon, and as a continuation of the improved – draughting programme, one of these 9Fs, No. 92178, was given a double blast pipe and chimney. Towards the end of January, 1958, No. 92178 commenced a series of Controlled Road Tests between Reading and Stoke Gifford. These showed that the double blast pipe and chimney saved fuel and gave an increase in power output. As a result, all new 9Fs, from No. 92183 onwards, were given double blast pipes and chimneys, and several of the earlier engines were also converted to the new arrangement.

215. Having left the train in Stoke Gifford yard, No. 92178 plus the dynamometer car and a bogie luggage van were in the process of turning on the Filton Junction triangle when I took this picture of them coming through the morning mist.

216.

After turning, No. 92178 took on water and coal (from weighed bags carried in the luggage van) before setting back on to her train in Stoke Gifford yard.

I always liked the 9Fs, but as I photographed No. 92178 standing in Stoke Gifford yard, I thought that she looked particularly striking. Then I suddenly realised why; – she was running without smoke deflectors.

**THE CONTROLLED ROAD TEST
ON 29th January, 1958.**

217. The test train standing in Stoke Gifford yard shortly before setting off on the return run to Reading.

218. As the departure time drew near for the return run, the morning mist had largely cleared, and No. 92178 made a splendid sight as she got her test train under way for the run to Reading.

PART 8

Branch Lines

I loved small country branch-lines. They always seemed to have about them such an air of serenity and unhurried ease; and when the two or three coach train happened to be hauled by an elderly tank engine that had been built many years ago by one of the pre-grouping companies, it was as if time had stood still.

But my kind of branch-line had no place in today's world of speed and "efficiency", and, alas, all my favourite lines have long since ceased to exist.

Over the past fifty years I have taken pictures on many different branch-lines, but I have decided to devote this section of the book to just four of my favourites —

    Axminster-Lyme Regis. (Ex-L & S.W.R.)
    Havant-Hayling Island. (Ex-L.B. & S.C.R.)
    Yatton-Clevedon. (Ex-G.W.R.)
    Evercreech Junction-Burnham-on-Sea. (Ex-S & D.J.R.)

219. Adams 4-4-2Ts Nos. 30584 and 30583 struggle up a very difficult stretch of 1 in 40 near Hartgrove farm, with the 4.36 p.m. from Axminster on a lovely summer afternoon in 1960.

> . . . to places
> Only dreamers know,
> Where the shy hare prints long paces,
> Where the night rooks go.
>
> *Thomas Hardy.*

HE AXMINSTER – LYME REGIS BRANCH

his seven-mile branch-line linked the seaside resort of Lyme Regis in Dorset, with the Jevonshire town of Axminster, on the old London and South Western main-line to 1e West of England. The line, which ran through enchanting country, abounded in 1arp curves, and had a ruling gradient of 1 in 40.

or years the branch had been worked by two ex-L & S.W.R. Adams 4-4-2 tank ngines, built in the 1880s, the bogie wheels of which had been given extra side-lay to suit the many sharp curves. From time to time several other types of engines ad been tried out to replace the ageing Adams tanks, but without success; either they amaged the track, or were insufficiently powerful to cope with the 1 in 40 gradients. o in 1946 the Southern Railway bought from the East Kent Railway an Adams 4-2T. which originally had been sold by the London and South Western Railway to 1e Government in 1917. This engine was given the increased side-play on the bogie heels, and then joined the other two Adams tanks on the branch.

ventually, in 1961, a suitable replacement for the old engines was found at last – an x-L.M.S. Ivatt 2-6-2T, was tried out and proved a success. So the long reign of the dams 4-4-2 tanks on the Axminster – Lyme Regis branch came to an end. Happily, o. 30583 has been preserved. Beautifully restored in L & S.W.R. livery and with her ld number 488, she is now running on the Bluebell Railway.

220. The 5.10p.m. Lyme Regis – Axminster sets off from Combpyne doubleheaded by Nos. 30583 and 30584. These two Adams tanks were not identical – note the difference in size of the trailing wheels and also the domes.

221. No. 30584 rounding a bend near Wyke Green with an Axminster – Lyme Regis train in the spring of 1960.

222.

On a beautiful spring morning in 1960, No. 30584 comes up through the trees near Bulmoor Cross with a train for Lyme Regis.

224. No. 30584 passing through the woods on Combpyne Hill with the 12.38 p.m. from Axminster on 6th June, 1960.

◄

223.

The 6th June had been a perfect summer's day, and with my friend Norman Lockett, I had spent it taking pictures on the branch. Normally after a session like this, I would have set off for home — 65 miles away in Bath — about 6p.m. but the day was turning into a glorious evening and we decided to wait and see the 6.45p.m. from Axminster.

It was a very still evening, and sitting in a field close to the line near Hartgrove farm, we heard the train coming from a long way off. To my excitement I suddenly realised from the beat that the train was double-headed. Gradually the sound of two hard-working engines drew nearer and nearer, and then Nos. 30584 and 30583 came slowly into sight, toiling up the 1 in 40 towards Hartgrove farm. In the low evening lighting the whole scene was superb — the perfect ending to a happy day.

225. The "Usurpers"! Two of the Ivatt 2-6-2 tanks, which finally ousted the Adams engines in 1961, crossing over Cannington viaduct with an enthusiast's special on 28th February, 1965.

226. Ex-L.B. & S.C. "Terrier" 0-6-0T. No. 32661, dwarfed by her two modern bogie coaches, sets off from Havant for Hayling Island in October, 1959.

THE HAVANT — HAYLING ISLAND BRANCH.

This four and a half mile line, built by the London, Brighton and South Coast Railway in 1867, linked Hayling Island with the main-line at Havant. Because of severe weight restrictions imposed by the swing bridge over the entrance to Langstone harbour, only very small engines could be used, and for years the line was worked by the little L.B. & S.C. 0-6-0 "Terrier" tanks. These had been designed in 1872 by William Stroudley. Many of them were subsequently rebuilt by D. Earle-Marsh with new boilers and extended smokeboxes.

It will be noticed that all the "Terriers" in these pictures are fitted with spark-arresters — a precaution against setting fire to the Langstone bridge which was largely built of wood!

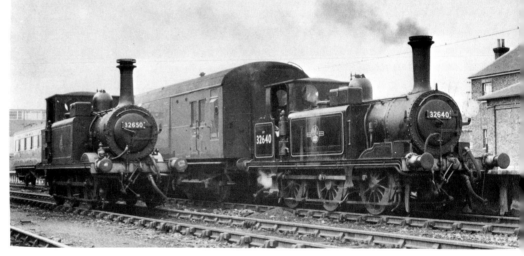

227. Two of the delightful little "Terriers" side by side at Havant in 1960. Happily, both are still in existence. No. 32650, preserved by the Borough of Sutton, is at present on loan to the Kent & East Sussex Railway Society at Rolvenden, whilst No. 32640 was bought by Butlins for display at their Pwllheli holiday camp. However, she has since been transferred to the Isle of Wight for preservation at the Haven Street Steam Centre. Although No. 32640 looks a little odd with a Drummond chimney in place of her original graceful Stroudley type, she is, in fact, one of the more famous "Terriers". Built in 1878, and numbered 40, she was given the name "Brighton", and the same year was sent to the Paris Exhibition, where she won a gold medal. In 1902 the London, Brighton and South Coast Railway sold No. 40 to the Isle of Wight Central Railway where she became No. 11, and eventually acquired the name "Newport". Then in 1947 the old engine was brought back to the mainland, and on the railways being nationalised, she was given back her old number, 40 — plus 32600.

228.

No. 32636 rounds the bend east of Havant station with a three-coach train for Hayling Island in September, 1963. No. 32636 is another "Terrier" that has been preserved; as No. 72 "Fenchurch", she is now running on the Bluebell Railway.

229.

On a crisp autumn morning in October 1959, No. 32661 has just crossed over the Langstone bridge on her way to Hayling Island with a two-coach train.

230.

No. 32650, on her way back from Hayling Island, draws near to Havant with an afternoon train in September, 1963.

THE YATTON — CLEVEDON BRANCH.

In 1847 the broad-gauge Bristol and Exeter Railway built a three and a half mile branch-line to connect the Somerset town of Clevedon, on the Bristol Channel, with Yatton, on the B. & E.R. main-line.

In contrast to another of my favourite branch-lines illustrated earlier, the Axminster — Lyme Regis, the Yatton — Clevedon branch was virtually level and had no curves of any consequence.

For many years in recent times, the service over the branch was operated largely by Railmotor trains, ex-G.W.R. motor-fitted 0-4-2Ts hauling trains from Yatton to Clevedon, and propelling them back in the reverse direction.

231. Ex-G.W.R. 0-4-2T. No. 1410 standing with her train in the bay platform on the west side of Yatton station.

232. A sad day. No. 1463 ready to leave Yatton, and waiting for the road, on Sunday, 7th August, 1960. This was the last day of steam on the branch. The next morning a diesel multiple unit took over the service.

233.

Another of the ex-G.W.R. 0-4-2Ts, No. 1426, bowling merrily along past an apple orchard in early summer, with her two-coach train for Clevedon.

234.

Return run. No. 1463 comes by, propelling her train from Clevedon to Yatton.

235.

With No. 1410 propelling in the rear, a train from Clevedon arrives back at Yatton. Just visible in the background is an Ivatt 2-6-2T. standing in the east bay platform with a train for the Cheddar Valley branch.

THE EVERCREECH JUNCTION — BURNHAM-ON-SEA BRANCH.*

The twenty-four miles of single-line which ran west from Evercreech Junction over to Burnham-on-Sea were part of the original main-line of the Somerset Central Railway and later, the Somerset and Dorset Railway. However, when the S & D opened their new line from Evercreech Junction up to Bath in 1874, this became the main-line, and the Evercreech Junction — Burnham-on-Sea section was relegated to being "The Branch".

For many years the branch was worked largely by two types of locomotive, both designed by S. W. Johnson — his attractive 1P 0-4-4 tanks and 3F 0-6-0 tender engines. (See also picture 409).

236. On a cold afternoon in April 1955 Johnson 1P 0-4-4T. No. 58086 sets off from Evercreech Junction with the 4.48 p.m. for Highbridge. As from November, 1951, passenger trains on the branch terminated at Highbridge, only the occasional summer excursions continuing to run right through over the final one and three quarter miles to Burnham-on-Sea station.

237. Three of S. W. Johnson's 0-4-4 tanks Nos. 58086, 58073 and 58051 standing outside Highbridge shed in the summer of 1953. All were ex-Midland engines, built towards the end of the last century.

238. Johnson 3F 0-6-0 No. 43194 arriving at Burnham-on-Sea with a three-coach local from Evercreech Junction. No. 43194 was built for the Somerset and Dorset at the Derby Works of the Midland Railway in 1896. Her original S & D number was 62.

239. When the Johnson tanks at last started to feel their age, the type that replaced them was Ivatt's 2-6-2T. design of 1946. On a sultry summer's day, No. 41291 is drifting down through Pylle woods with the 1.15p.m. from Evercreech Junction to Highbridge.

More pictures of this branch appear in my book "The Somerset and Dorset – an English Cross-Country Railway", published by the Oxford Publishing Company.

PART 9
Industrial Engines

Industrial engines had a character and charm all their own. Many firms in Britain used to specialise in building steam locomotives for industrial service, and most of these manufacturers had their own distinctive design features. One glimpse of an industrial engine was often all that was necessary to identify immediately the builder.

It was this wonderful variety of engines that I found so fascinating, and every year I used to try and spend at least one week of my holidays visiting industrial lines. Two of my friends, Norman Lockett and the Rev. Alan Newman, share my love of these engines, and we went on many happy 'industrial' expeditions together; but the one that will always stand out in my memory, was the week we spent in early May 1960 visiting some twenty-three ironstone lines in the East Midlands. In perfect weather, we saw a wonderful variety of engines, many of them in immaculate condition, and all working in delightful country surroundings.

Over the years that I visited industrial lines, I was always received with courtesy and I am exceedingly grateful to the many firms and organisations who so kindly gave me permission to take pictures of their steam locomotives.

240. Two of my friends who share my love of industrial engines, the Rev. Alan Newman (left) and Norman Lockett. On a fine but cold morning in March 1962 we were on our way over to the Scaldwell and Kettering ironstone lines, when we saw this elderly narrow gauge Andrew Barclay 0-6-0T. sitting in a yard beside a garage on the outskirts of Chipping Norton.

241. Another friend who accompanied us on many of our 'industrial' expeditions was the Rev. Teddy Boston – an ardent steam enthusiast (see picture 398). On 13th May, 1964, in rather appropriate surroundings, the Rev. Boston passes by Linby church, riding on the footplate of "Peter", an 0-6-0ST. built by Hunslet in 1943. "Peter", an N.C.B. locomotive, was on the way, light engine, to Linby Colliery.

IRONSTONE RAILWAYS.

Most ironstone quarries were situated in the heart of the countryside, and had their own line connecting them with British Railways. These lines, running along the edge of fields, and sometimes through small woods, were some of the most delightful and attractive industrial railways in the whole of England.

For the pleasure of having seen many of these ironstone lines, I owe a tremendous debt to Eric Tonks, for I did not even know of the existence of some of the more remote and attractive lines until the publication of his outstanding book on the ironstone tramways of the Midlands.

242. STOREFIELD IRONSTONE QUARRIES. Although the line connecting these quarries with the B.R. main line was under one and a half miles long, it included a charming stretch through the heart of a small wood, and also a very steep climb up to the B.R. exchange sidings. Standing side by side at the foot of the incline up to B.R. are 0-4-0ST. "Cockspur", Peckett, 1289/1912, and 0-4-0ST. No. 11, Andrew Barclay, 1047/1905.

43. OXFORDSHIRE IRONSTONE QUARRIES. These quarries, situated near Wroxton, had one of the most efficiently run rail systems of all the ironstone quarries I visited. The line leading to B.R. was over three miles long, and double track; right-hand running was practised, due to the siting of the crushing plant.

In this picture, 0-6-0T. No. 1, "Sir Thomas", Hudswell Clarke, 1334/1918, is climbing towards Wroxton with a train of empty iron ore tippler wagons. The signal guarded a level-crossing over the Wroxton-Hanwell road, and was worked from a signal box situated beside the crossing.

244.
0-6-0ST. "Lamport No.2", W.G. Bagnall, 2669/1942, crosses over the Scaldwell-Brixworth road as she propels a rake of steel side-tipping "dump cars" towards the exchange point with the narrow gauge system.

SCALDWELL IRONSTONE QUARRIES*. The rail system serving these Northamptonshire quarries was most interesting, being a combination of standard gauge and narrow gauge (see picture 395). The ore was brought out from the quarries in small 3ft. gauge wooden wagons and transported for a little under two miles to an exchange point with the standard gauge. At this exchange point, the narrow gauge ran in above the level of the standard gauge, so it was quite a simple matter for the ore to be transhipped from the small wooden wagons down a chute into the steel "dump-cars" waiting below. The ore was then carried a further two and a half miles down to the calcining clamps beside the B.R. sidings just south of Lamport.

245.

Another of the standard gauge engines 0-6-0ST. "Robert", Avonside, 2068/1933, passes by on her way down to the B.R. sidings.

*Many pictures of the Scaldwell narrow gauge system appear in my book "The Narrow Gauge Charm of Yesterday", published by the Oxford Publishing Company.

EXTON PARK MINES. The deposits of ironstone in this part of Rutland are rather deeper under the surface, and some of the ore at Exton Park is mined, not quarried. The rail system serving these workings is very extensive and second in size only to Corby (see pictures 248/50). When I visited the line in 1960 there were eight 0-6-0ST. locomotives at Exton Park. All were built post-war by the Yorkshire Engine Company; five, to the Company's own design, had outside cylinders, and the remaining three were the M.o.S. "Austerity" design with inside cylinders. The outside cylinder engines were painted apple green, lined out dark green with a yellow edge, and had red coupling rods. The "Austerity" engines were maroon, lined-out with red and yellow. All the engines were in immaculate condition and an absolute joy to behold.

246. 0-6-0ST. No. 36, Yorkshire Engine Company, 2489/1950, setting back into one of the quarries to pick up some loaded wagons.

247.
Exton Park is in a beautiful setting – in this picture a train of ore, hauled by 0-6-0 ST. No. 11 (YE 2568/1954) is coming up to the level-crossing over the very lovely tree-lined Barnsdale Avenue.

248. One of the large Robert Stephenson & Hawthorns 0-6-0STs. No. 56, 7667/1950, draws near to Corby with a train of modern steel hopper wagons carrying a heavy load of iron ore.

CORBY QUARRIES. This vast complex of ironstone quarries lies on the eastern outskirts of the steel-making town of Corby, and is served by the largest 'ironstone' railway in Britain which carries the ore direct from the quarries to the steelworks. When I last visited the system in the early 1960s — before 'dieselisation' had set in — there were some sixty steam locomotives in use. All were maintained in first-class mechanical and external condition, and reflected great credit on the locomotive superintendent, Mr. Bates.

249.
0-6-0ST. No. 39, "Rhos", Hudswell Clarke, 1308/1918.

250.
Two generations of 0-6-0 saddle-tanks — No. 34, "Calettwr", Manning Wardle, 1316/1895, and No. 63, Robert Stephenson & Hawthorns, 7761/1954.

SOME "IRONSTONE" ENGINES

— with their builder's name, number and date of manufacture.

251. HARLAXTON MINES. 0-6-0ST. "Curzon", Hunslet, 422/1887, with an old L & N.W.R. six-wheeled brake van.

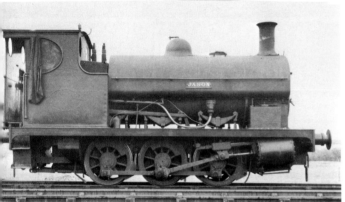

252. BUCKMINSTER QUARRIES. 0-6-0ST. "Jason", Robert Stephenson, 3170/1905.

253. MARKET OVERTON QUARRIES. 0-6-0ST "Adderley", Avonside, 1694/1915.

254. BYFIELD QUARRIES. 0-6-0ST "Cherwell", Bagnall, 2654/1942.

255. CHARWELTON QUARRIES. 0-4-0ST No. 8, Yorkshire Engine Co., 784/1905.

256. BUCKMINSTER QUARRIES. 0-6-0ST "Sewstern", Andrew Barclay, 2314/1951.

257. BYFIELD QUARRIES. 0-6-0ST "Sir Berkeley", Manning Wardle, 1210/1890

SUGAR FACTORY.

In Norfolk there used to be an enchanting line, the Wissington Light Railway, which served an extensive area of farming country south of Stoke Ferry. All that now remains of this splendidly rural railway is one and a half miles of line linking the British Sugar Corporation factory at Wissington, with B.R. at Abbey, on the old Great Eastern Stoke Ferry branch. Before the arrival of the inevitable diesel, the B.S.C. used three attractive 0-6-0 steam locomotives to work the line, two Manning Wardles and a Hudswell Clarke.

258. The British Sugar Corporation's three 0-6-0ST steam locomotives at Wissington. "Wissington", Hudswell Clarke, 1700/1938, and the two Manning Wardles, "Newcastle", 1532/1901 and 2006/1921. As a fire precaution, all three engines were fitted with wire-globe spark arresters.

259.
Crossing the imposing concrete bridge over the New Fen Drainage Cut — "Wissington" on her way back, light engine, from Abbey to the factory.

260.
"Wissington" passing through the fenland countryside with a train for the exchange sidings at Abbey.

STONE QUARRY.

This large stone quarry is at Whatley near Frome, in Somerset. Originally the line between the quarry and the ex-G.W.R. North Somerset branch had been narrow gauge, but during the 1939-45 war this was converted to standard gauge. Recently, under the new owners, Amey Roadstone Corporation, the line has been much improved and realigned, and is now worked by main-line diesels.

In the 1950s, the motive power was steam; — four vertical boiler, geared, Sentinels and an 0-4-0 Andrew Barclay saddle-tank. But by the late 1960s, the steam locomotives had gone, replaced by new Sentinel diesels.

261. One of the rather unorthodox, vertical boiler, geared Sentinels, No. 1, 9374/1947, shunting wagons in the exchange sidings at Hapsford.

262. After 1949, the only "orthodox" steam locomotive on the line was 0-4-0ST "Medway", Andrew Barclay, 969/1903. She was necessarily of rather squat appearance, because of severely limited head room under a road bridge. This picture, taken in October 1955, was the last time I saw "Medway"; she was scrapped early the following year.

GASWORKS.

BATH.

263. Bath Gasworks, with its own compact rail system, was situated on the north side of the main-line at Bath Junction. To carry out their shunting, the Gas Board had two diminutive saddle-tanks, and whenever I was taking photographs at Bath Junction, I always hoped there might be the opportunity to obtain a picture of one of these little saddle-tanks standing alongside a Somerset and Dorset engine; but it was not to be. The little Gasworks engines were most elusive, and normally all one saw of them was a tantalising column of steam rising above a building, or a wispy trail of smoke passing behind a rake of wagons. In this picture, taken outside their shed, the engine on the left is Avonside 1978/1928, whilst the smaller engine is Peckett 1267/1912.

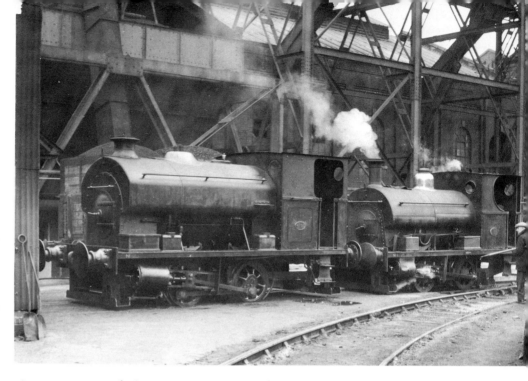

BECKTON.

264. No. 1 of the By-products department engines. Built in 1892, she was a Neilson engine, maker's number 4444. Behind her stands No. 9, built by Peckett in 1920, maker's number 1874.

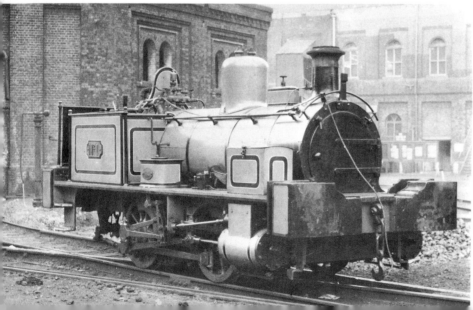

265. Beckton Gasworks had a fascinating stud of locomotives. Because of the many sharp curves and very limited head-room, all were short wheelbase 0-4-0s, devoid of any cab. The livery of the Gasworks engines was green, whilst those used in the By-products department were painted maroon. This is Gasworks engine No. 1, Neilson 1561/1870. Note the interesting feature of outside Stephenson valve gear.

266.
The Stavely Iron & Chemical Company Ltd., had some interesting engines, including two 0-4-0 saddle-tanks built by Markham & Company of Chesterfield — a firm not widely associated with the building of steam locomotives. This is "Gladys", built by Markham in 1894, maker's number 109.

IRONWORKS.

267. Amongst the steam locomotives used at their Stanton works by Stanton & Stavely Ltd., were some intriguing 0-4-0 crane-tanks. These were made by Andrew Barclay, and in this picture No. 34 (2037/1937) is in the process of unloading pipes.

SHIPBUILDING.

268. William Doxford & Son Ltd, used several crane-tank locomotives at their Pallion shipyard in Sunderland. Standing outside their shed at the end of the day's work are — "Southwick" and "Millfield", both built by Robert Stephenson & Hawthorns in 1942, maker's numbers 7069 and 7070, and "Pallion" built by Hawthorn Leslie in 1902, maker's number 2517.

269. Before being ousted by a diesel, this small 0-4-0 well-tank was used by the Fairfield Shipbuilding Company at Chepstow. The engine was built by Kerr, Stuart in 1918, maker's number 3063.

DOCKS AND HARBOURS.

270.

DAGENHAM DOCK. In pre-diesel days Samuel Williams & Sons Ltd. operated a most interesting variety of steam locomotives at Dagenham Dock. These two are elderly Manning Wardles — No. 4 built in 1877, maker's number 641, and No. 7, built in 1885, maker's number 951.

271.

AVONMOUTH DOCKS. In the days of steam, the shunting at Avonmouth Docks was carried out by a stud of 0-6-0 saddle-tanks built by the two Bristol firms of Peckett and Avonside. Standing outside their shed are S10 "Hallen", Peckett 2035/1943 and two Avonsides, S4 "Percy" 1800/1918 and S5 "Brian", 1799/1918.

272.

SEAHAM HARBOUR.This fascinating little 0-4-0 saddle-tank was built by Stephen Lewin, of Poole, Dorset, in 1863. Some idea of her size may be judged by the N.C.B. wagon to which she is coupled. Long after the rest of the steam locomotives had been replaced by diesels, the Seaham Harbour Dock Company continued to use this diminutive steam locomotive because her very low overall height permitted her to pass beneath the coal staithes and so reach lines inaccessible to the diesels.

273.
Locomotives standing outside their shed at the end of the day's work.

A BREWERY RAILWAY.

To service their vast brewery complex in Burton-on-Trent, Bass, Ratcliff & Gretton Ltd. operated a very fine railway system. The network of lines totalled some sixteen miles, and in addition, the Company's engines had running powers over ten miles of British Railways with which the system was integrated — and all this within the confines of Burton-on-Trent. The Bass, Ratcliff & Gretton engines were 0-4-0 saddle-tanks, as were those of their associate company, Worthington & Company Ltd., which also used the system. Bass engines were painted turkey red, and the Worthington engines were dark blue. All were kept in absolutely splendid condition.

Members of the Bath Railway Society used to make an annual expedition to see this outstanding private railway system. The train journey up to Burton-on-Trent was always a jolly affair — we used to catch the 7.23 a.m. local from Bath, Green Park, over to Mangotsfield, where we would join the northbound express which had left Bristol at 7.35 a.m.

On our arrival at the Brewery at about 11.30a.m. we would first of all be ushered into the sampling room to revive ourselves after the journey. (Great care had to be exercised at this stage of the visit, or one's focusing ability would be impaired for the rest of the day!) Then we would board the Company's Visitors' Saloon — a splendid four-wheeled coach — and be taken for a tour of the system. The hospitality which we always received from Bass, Ratcliff & Gretton Ltd. was almost overwhelming and I know that many of the older members of the Bath Railway Society who came on these expeditions, share my feeling of gratitude to the Company for the tremendous pleasure we derived from these visits.

274. 0-4-0ST. No. 11, built by Neilson, Reid in 1899, maker's number 5568, standing at Shobnall Maltings with the Visitors' Saloon on 21st May, 1960, during a visit by members of the Bath Railway Society.

In the background, an ex-L.M.S. 0-6-0T. is passing by an old Midland signal box, several of which were dotted around on the B.R. sections of the system.

275. Bass engines by two different manufacturers — No. 2, built in 1900 by Neilson, Reid, maker's number 5760, and No.3, built in 1890 by Thornewill & Warham, a firm not widely known as manufacturers of steam locomotives. The wheels of the Thornewill & Warham engines were slightly larger in diameter than those of the Neilson, Reid engines.

276. No. 3, the Thornewill & Warham engine, standing by an old Midland bracket signal. She was waiting to pass over one of the several street crossings in the heart of Burton-on-Trent.

277. Worthington engine No. 15, built by Hudswell, Clarke in 1901, maker's number 602.

COLLIERIES.

Until quite recently there was tremendous variety in the vast fleet of steam locomotives operated by the National Coal Board. Amongst their stock were engines of all ages and by many different manufacturers, and a visit to a colliery system was always full of interest. Over the years, I have been to many different collieries and I am exceedingly grateful to the N.C.B. for their kindness in allowing me to take pictures of their steam locomotives.

278. MEASHAM. By the very nature of the industry, collieries are bound to be dirty and dusty places, and yet a surprisingly large number of N.C.B. steam locomotives were kept in excellent condition. These two immaculate engines at Measham Colliery are outstanding examples of how some N.C.B. engines were looked after. The 0-6-0ST. was built by W.G. Bagnall in 1954, maker's number 3061, and the 0-4-0ST. was a Hudswell, Clarke of 1952, maker's number 1832.

279. BADDESLEY. One of the N.C.B.'s most interesting locomotives was this Garratt, "William Francis", used at Baddesley Colliery. She was built by Beyer, Peacock in 1937, maker's number 6841.

EX-MAIN-LINE ENGINES IN N.C.B. SERVICE.

Before the nationalisation of the coal industry, Collieries had quite often bought from main-line companies, engines which had become redundant. The N.C.B. continued this practice to a limited extent, acquiring, for example, several of the Hawksworth Pannier Tanks from the Western Region of B.R.

281. WALKDEN. Amongst the stud of locomotives employed on this N.C.B. system were several ex-North Staffordshire Railway 0-6-2Ts which had been bought by the Lancashire Associated Collieries in the mid-'thirties. One of these engines, No. 2, had been restored to her old North Staffordshire livery for an exhibition.

280. RAWNSLEY. 0-6-0T. "Cannock Wood" was an ex-London, Brighton & South Coast Railway engine built at Brighton Works in 1877. Since entering colliery service she had acquired a rather ugly replacement chimney and also small side-windows in the cab. Behind the brake van is 0-6-0ST. "Progress", built by Peckett in 1899, maker's number 786.

282.

LITTLETON. The N.C.B. also made use of ex-main-line brake vans. This old Great Western van was employed on the Littleton system, and was being taken down to the exchange sidings by 0-6-0ST. "Robert Nelson No. 4", built by Hunslet in 1936, maker's number 1800.

283. 0-6-2T. No. 42, built by Robert Stephenson in 1920, maker's number 3801, standing outside the main running shed.

PHILADELPHIA. This large N.C.B. motive power depot was on the former Lambton Collieries Railway in Co. Durham.

284. The method of coaling engines at Philadelphia was simple and efficient. From hopper wagons standing on an overhead stage, coal was discharged down chutes into the bunkers of locomotives waiting below. In this picture the leading engine, 0-6-2T. No. 52, was originally owned by the Taff Vale Railway in South Wales. She was built by Neilson Reid in 1899, maker's number 5408. Behind her stands 0-6-0ST. No. 8, a Robert Stephenson & Hawthorns of 1952, maker's number 7691.

285. HAUNCHWOOD. – "Engines of all ages". Leading this trio of saddle-tanks is 0-6-0 "Good Luck", built by Hunslet in 1890, maker's number 498. Next comes 0-4-0 "Success", built by Andrew Barclay in 1909, maker's number 1167. Bringing up the rear is 0-6-0 No. 1, a Hunslet of 1955, maker's number 3828.

286. DONISTHORPE. – "Immaculate steam". 0-6-0ST. "No. 2 Phoenix", built by Hawthorn, Leslie in 1905, maker's number 2611, gleams in the sunshine outside her shed on a lovely spring morning in 1964.

287. GROVE. 0-6-0ST. No.3, Peckett, 618/1895.

288. WALSALL WOOD. 0-6-0ST., No. 5, "Lord Kitchener", Kitson, 5158/1915.

289. BESTWOOD. 0-6-0ST. "Valerie", Hawthorn Leslie, 3606/1924.

290. NEWDIGATE. 0-6-0T. "Coventry No. 1", North British, 24564/ 1939.

291. ARLEY. 0-6-0ST. "Joan", Avonside, 2048/1932.

292. MEASHAM. 0-6-0ST., "Progress", Robert Stephenson & Hawthorns, 7298/1946.

293. NORTON HILL. 0-4-0T., Hunslet, 1684/1931.

294. GEDLING. 0-6-0ST, "Catherine", Andrew Barclay, 1000/1903.

and their maker's name, number and building date.

295. LAMBTON. 0-6-2T. No. 31, Kitson, 4533/1907.

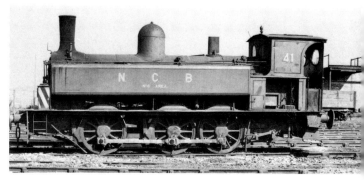

296. DERWENTHAUGH. 0-6-0PT. No. 41, Kitson, 2510/1883.

297. ARLEY. 0-6-0ST. "Coventry No. 4", Peckett, 1745/1927.

298. COPPICE. 0-6-0T. No. 2, Kitson, 5358/1921.

299. LITTLETON. 0-6-0ST., "Littleton No. 5", Manning Wardle, 2018/1922.

300. MOUNTAIN ASH. 0-6-0ST. "Sir John", Avonside, 1680/1914.

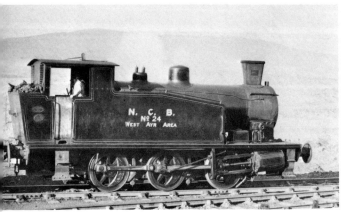

301. WATERSIDE. 0-6-0T. No. 24, Andrew Barclay, 2335/1953.

302. COPPICE. 0-6-0ST. No. 3, "Hanbury", Peckett 567/1894.

303. TWERTON. Ex-G.W.R. 4-6-0 No. 4091 "Dudley Castle", with the 5.00p.m. down stopping train from Swindon, has just emerged from Twerton tunnel on the western outskirts of Bath. For a close-up of this attractive tunnel mouth, see picture 459.

PART 10
Interesting and Attractive Locations

TUNNELS

I am happy watching trains anywhere, but in the days of steam there used to be some locations which I found particularly attractive. I loved the sight of a steam engine bursting out of a tunnel — climbing a steep gradient — crossing a high viaduct — picking up water. The next few pages show some of the scenes I enjoyed in the days of steam.

304. CATESBY. 9F 2-10-0 No. 92013, hauling a heavy coal train, plods slowly out of the southern end of Catesby tunnel, on the old Great Central main-line to London.

305.

HONITON. The eastern end of Honiton tunnel was an enchanting spot. The line emerged into a deep, wooded cutting, and with the nearest road over half a mile away, there was little to disturb the peace and serenity of these beautiful surroundings. Just emerging into the sunshine is the 10.30a.m. (SO) Ilfracombe to Waterloo, hauled by S.R. Pacific No. 34086, "219 Squadron".

Two Tunnels on the Southern Main-Line to the West of England.

Although the scenery at these two spots is still as beautiful as ever, this once magnificent main-line is now but a shadow of its former self. After falling under the control of the Western Region, the line was singled west of Salisbury, and as much traffic as possible was diverted away to run over former Great Western routes.

306. BUCKHORN WESTON. Another attractive setting where I spent many happy hours, was the eastern end of Buckhorn Weston tunnel. Climbing away from the tunnel in September, 1961, is one of Bulleid's rebuilt Pacifics, No. 34096 "Trevone", with the 8.09a.m. (SO) Torrington to Waterloo.

307. CHIPPING NORTON. Making a cautious exit from the southern end of Chipping Norton tunnel is ex-G.W.R. 2-6-2T. No. 4106.

TUNNELS.

308. BRADFORD-ON-AVON. Ex-G.W.R. 4-6-0 No. 6849 "Walton Grange" bursts out of Bradford-on-Avon tunnel with an up Sunday parcels train in the spring of 1961.

309. SODBURY. The up "Red Dragon", hauled by ex-G.W.R. 4-6-0 No. 4081 "Warwick Castle", comes up through the deep and very steep-sided cutting leading away from the eastern end of Sodbury tunnel on the Paddington–South Wales main-line.

310.

BINCOMBE. The Sunday 10.12a.m. from Bournemouth, in the charge of S.R. Pacific No. 34086 "219 Squadron", drifts out of Bincombe tunnel and down the bank towards Weymouth.

311. FOX'S WOOD. On a warm afternoon in late spring 1960, ex-G.W.R. 4-6-0 No. 1011 "County of Chester", passes over the troughs as she heads east with the 12.50 p.m. Cardiff to Brighton.

WATERTROUGHS.

312. Eeek! ex-G.W.R. 2-6-0 No. 5387, in charge of a westbound goods, slightly over-does it!

313. CHARLBURY. Ex-G.W.R. 4-6-0 No. 5054 "Earl of Ducie", takes water from Charlbury troughs whilst in charge of an Oxford University Railway Society Special in May 1964.

314. SODBURY. A near thing! A down goods — seen disappearing westwards — nearly prevented my getting this picture of ex-G.W.R. 4-6-0 No. 6028 "King George VI" taking water from Sodbury troughs as she approached Sodbury tunnel with the up "Red Dragon".

BRIDGES.

315. CRAWFORD. 9F. 2-10-0 No. 92233 rumbles over the Clyde at Crawford with a northbound train of coal empties.

VIADUCTS

317. RIBBLEHEAD. This magnificent viaduct, on the Settle-Carlisle line, has twenty-four arches — the highest 165 feet above ground level — and took four years to build. The goods train coming north over the viaduct is hauled by "Britannia" Pacific No. 70010 "Owen Glendower".

318. DOCKER. A Stanier "Black Five" drifts down over the Docker viaduct as she heads south towards Oxenholme with a long train of empty wagons.

◄

316.

MENAI STRAIT. Ex-L.M.S. "Jubilee" class 4-6-0 No. 45643 "Rodney", in charge of a Holyhead — London meat train, leaves the Britannia Tubular Bridge over the Menai Strait. This historic bridge, designed by Robert Stephenson and opened in 1850, has recently been rebuilt after suffering severe damage by fire. The rebuilding has changed considerably the appearance of the bridge, but happily the lions at each end have survived.

INCLINES

SHAP.

319. Early one morning in April, 1966, Stanier "Black Five" No. 45449 plods uphill towards Greenholme in a biting east wind, with a north bound goods. Banking strenuously in the rear is 2-6-4T. No. 42210.

320. In the late afternoon of 11th August, 1967, 9F 2-10-0 No. 92033, going extremely well, thunders up past Shap Wells with a heavy bulk ammonia train, assisted in the rear by B.R. class "4" No. 75037.

321. UPWEY. In May, 1967, two of Bulleid's Pacifics climb the bank out of Weymouth with the 6.15p.m. for Waterloo. The leading engine, "West Country" No. 34023, is still in original condition, whilst the train engine is a rebuilt "Merchant Navy", No. 35030.

322. BREWHAM. Ex-G.W.R. 4-6-0 No. 6945 "Glasfryn Hall" making a spirited climb of Brewham bank with a Weymouth — Paddington train on a warm evening in early August, 1956.

THE LICKEY INCLINE.

This famous incline, one of the steepest on any British main-line, lies on the old Midland route between Bristol and Birmingham. From Bromsgrove the line climbs for two miles on a gradient of 1 in 37.7 up to the summit at Blackwell. In the days of steam, virtually every north-bound train would stop at Bromsgrove for one or more bankers to come on at the rear and assist up to Blackwell.

323. Banking engines waiting at the foot of the incline at Bromsgrove to assist trains up to Blackwell.

324. Tragedy came early to the Lickey Incline; on 10th November, 1840, shortly after the line had been opened, the boiler of a banking engine blew up, killing the two enginemen. On their memorial stones, which may still be seen in Bromsgrove churchyard, is carved a bas-relief of an American-designed Norris 4-2-0, several of which were in use on the line at the time. However, it was not one of these engines which was responsible for killing the enginemen, but an experimental locomotive designed by Dr. Church.

325. A banker, 0-6-0PT. No. 8404, coming on to the rear of the 7.35a.m. ex-Bristol, to give assistance from Bromsgrove up to Blackwell. Although a Swindon design of 1947, No. 8404 was not, strictly speaking, an ex-Great Western engine, having been built in 1949 after the railways of Britain had been nationalised.

326. After bringing a northbound express to a stand for rear-end assistance, 9F. 2-10-0 No. 92104 gets her train under way again with vigour as she comes through Bromsgrove station towards the start of the Lickey Incline.

THE LICKEY INCLINE

327. The up "Pines Express" coming slowly up the incline on a hot day in late summer, 1959. The train engine, a B.R. standard Caprotti class 5, No. 73138, did not sound as if she was trying very hard — most of the work appeared to be being done in the rear! (see picture 329).

328. For many years, rear-end assistance up the Lickey was provided by the famous Midland Railway 0-10-0 "Lickey Banker", and a stud of ex-L.M.S. 3F. 0-6-0 tanks. However, on the line passing into the control of the Western Region in 1958, ex-Great Western type locomotives began to make their appearance. In 1959, one of the ex-G.W.R. engines being tried out was this 2-8-0T. No. 5226.

329.

After the Midland 0-10-0 was withdrawn from service, a B.R. standard 9F. 2-10-0 was usually included in the stud of bankers stationed at Bromsgrove. In this picture, 9F. 2-10-0 No. 92231 and ex-L.M.S. 3F. 0-6-0T. No. 47308 are giving rear-end assistance to the up "Pines Express".

330. At the end of the two miles of 1 in 37.7, 9F, 2-10-0 No. 92155 finally breasts the summit at Blackwell with her northbound freight.

331. With the climb of the Lickey Incline completed, a northbound express, hauled by 9F. 2-10-0 No. 92164, gathers speed through Blackwell station.

332. — and the two banking engines, 0-6-0PTs Nos. 8401 and 8404, drop away in the rear.

SOUTH OF SUNDERLAND.

A multiple of tracks ran close beside the sea south of Sunderland. Over this busy section of line passed a constant flow of empty wagons on their way to the collieries, and full trains of coal coming back in. I never had any luck with the weather at this most interesting location until my last visit on 13th June, 1967, when, on a perfect summer evening, I was treated to a virtual procession of trains passing by, hauled by ex-North Eastern Railway J.27 0-6-0s and Q.6 0-8-0s.

333. Ex-North Eastern Railway J.27 0-6-0 No. 65795 heading south with empties for Silksworth colliery.

334. Another long train of empty wagons sets off south hauled by ex-N.E.R. Q.6 0-8-0 No. 63458.

QUAY TRAMWAYS.

335. Ex-L & S.W.R. B4 0-4-0T. No. 30093, shunting vans on Poole Quay on a fine evening in early August, 1954, passes by the paddle steamer "Embassy".

336. With much caution, ex-G.W.R. 0-6-0 Pannier Tank No. 7780 hauls her train at walking pace along Weymouth Quay.

337. 9F 2-10-0 No. 92019 sets off south from the wilds of Blea Moor with the up "Long Meg" — a train of anhydrite which ran regularly to Widnes.

THE SETTLE & CARLISLE.

This very beautiful stretch of railway should really have come in under the section "Favourite Lines", for there are so many places on this magnificently engineered line that I find quite superb. Trying to choose pictures for these two pages has, frankly, defeated me; at different times I must have selected over twenty pictures "which just cannot be left out" — but, sadly, space has decreed otherwise. (However, two more pictures, 317 and 471 have been squeezed in under different sections.)

▶

339. With Wild Boar Fell in the background, Stanier "Black Five" No. 44669 brings her Carlisle — Skipton goods towards the summit at Ais Gill, 1169 feet above sea level.

THE CLIMB TO AIS GILL.

338. Ex-L.M.S. "Jubilee" class 4-6-0 No. 45593 "Kolhapur", climbing up through the Mallerstang valley with a southbound freight.

340. Standing together outside the shed — two 4-6-0s, "Black Five" No. 44851 and "Jubilee" class 6P No. 45662 "Kempenfelt", and a class 5MT 2-6-0, Horwich "Crab" No. 42890.

PART 11

Engine Sheds

The first engine shed I visited was Bath Road Depot, Bristol, in September, 1925, and I shall never forget the thrill of that occasion. That was over fifty years ago, and since then I have visited innumerable sheds throughout Great Britain, but right up to the end of steam, this sense of excitement whenever I entered a shed, never left me.

In the space allotted to "Engine Sheds", there is only room to illustrate a handful of the sheds I knew, and trying to decide which should be the "chosen few" has been extremely difficult!

BRISTOL, BARROW ROAD
(Ex-Midland Railway)

341.

"Patriot" class 6P 4-6-0 No. 45504 "Royal Signals" drifts down the bank past Barrow Road shed with the 7.00 a.m. Sheffield to Bristol.

342. When day is done — steam locomotives resting in Barrow Road shed in the evening at the end of their day's work.

343. A general view of the west end of Eastleigh Shed in May 1953. On the left are ex-S.R. Bulleid Pacific No. 34108 "Wincanton" and ex-L.M.S. Fairburn 2-6-4T. No. 42096. Then come two ex-L & S.W.R. Drummond M7 0-4-4Ts Nos. 30378 and 30379, and next to these is a new B.R. standard class 4 2-6-0 No. 76008. On the right is another M7 0-4-4T, No. 30030.

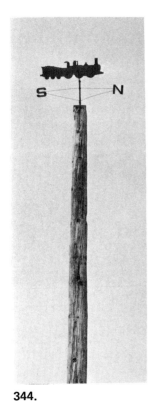

EASTLEIGH.

This large shed adjoined the old London and South Western Railway — later, Southern Railway — Works at Eastleigh.

345. Three new B.R. standard locomotives lined up beside the coaling stage in May 1953. The leading engines are class 4s—2-6-4T. No. 80032, built at Brighton in 1951, and 2-6-0 No. 76013, built at Horwich in 1952. Bringing up the rear is class 3 2-6-2T. No. 82015, built at Swindon in 1951.

344.
A happy touch — the weathercock outside the foreman's office, in the shape of an old L&SWR engine.

346. A line of five engines standing outside the eastern end of the shed. The leading engine is ex-S.R. "King Arthur" class 4-6-0 No. 30786 "Sir Lionel", then come two tanks, ex-L & S.W.R. 02 class 0-4-4T, No. 30193 designed by Adams in 1889, and an ex-L.M.S. Ivatt 2-6-2T. No. 41304 of 1946. Next to these is an unidentified B.R. standard class 4 2-6-0 and, at the tail end, a diminutive ex-L & S.W.R. class B4 0-4-0T. No. 30082, built by Drummond early this century to an Adams design of 1891.

347. Two ex-S.R. "Lord Nelson" class 4-6-0s, No. 30861 "Lord Anson" and No. 30858 "Lord Dun-can". These engines were designed by Maunsell in 1926. Later modifications by Bulleid included the fitting of multiple-jet blast pipes and large-diameter chimneys.

348.

D.S. 680, one of Stroud-ley's little L.B. & S.C.R. 0-6-0 "Terrier" tanks at Eastleigh in October 1960. D.S. 680 – original L.B. & S.C.R. No. 54 – was built in 1875, and ended her active life as service locomotive at the carriage and wagon works at Lancing. She is now preserved at Montreal Railway Historical Museum, Canada. (For more "Terriers", see pictures 226-230, and 350).

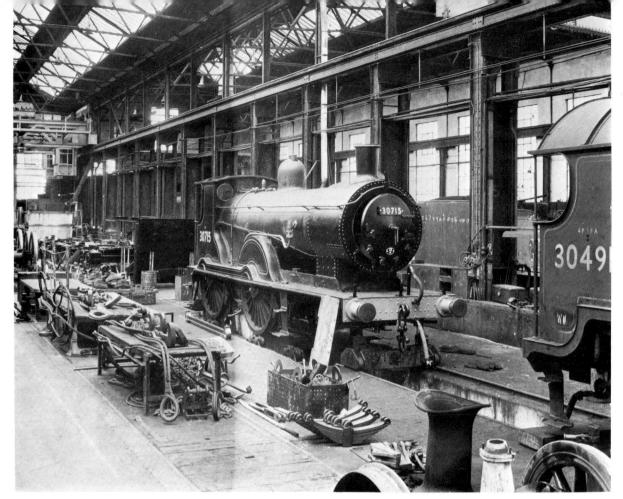

349. Ex–L. & S.W.R. Drummond T9 4-4-0 No. 30715 being overhauled in April 1959.

EASTLEIGH WORKS.

350. In October 1960, one of the ex-L.B. & S.C.R. Stroudley "Terriers", No. 82 "Boxhill", was in the process of being completely reconditioned and restored to her original resplendent livery, prior to preservation by British Railways.

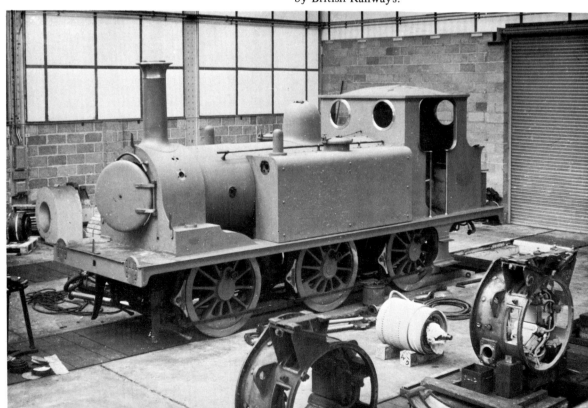

351. Ex-L.B. & S.C.R. K class 2-6-0 No. 32348, an L.B. Billinton design of 1913. Behind her stands one of R.J. Billinton's L.B. & S.C.R. designs, class E4 0-6-2T. No. 32562.

EASTLEIGH —
Locomotives
Ex-Works.

One of the pleasures of a visit to Eastleigh was the number of interesting engines one would see in immaculate condition, just ex-Works.

352. This little 0-4-0T. No. 77s, was used for many years by the Engineer's Department at Redbridge Sleeper Depot. She started off life in 1907 as one of Drummond's motor-train 2-2-0Ts, and was converted to an 0-4-0T. in 1913.

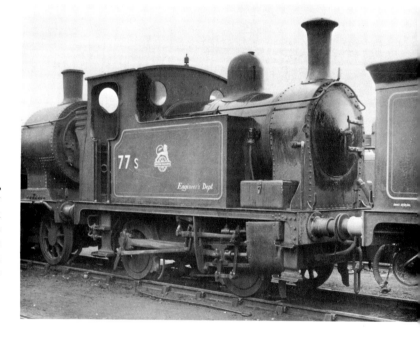

353.

8F No. 30494, one of the massive ex-L. & S.W.R. G16 class 4-8-0Ts designed by Urie in 1921 for shunting the "Hump" marshalling yard at Feltham. Only four of these impressive locomotives were built.

BRISTOL, ST. PHILIP'S MARSH.

This was one of two large Great Western sheds at Bristol.

354. Western Region motive power personalities in May, 1964 — plus a couple of "Castles". From the left, Arthur Macarthy, Running Inspector; Harold Morris, Shed-master, Bath; Jack Hancock, Chief Divisional Running Inspector; and Victor Smith, Assistant to Shed-master, Bristol. The "Castles" are No. 5054 "Earl of Ducie", and No. 7032 "Denbigh Castle."

355. – Mainly B.R. 9F 2-10-0s and ex- L.M.S. and WD 2-8-0s.

356. Standing in line next to the coal stage road, two ex-G.W.R. 2-8-0s Nos. 3803 and 2859, an unidentified 2-6-0, and WD 2-8-0 No. 90179.

357. Sunday morning at St. Philip's Marsh – a quiet assembly of tanks, plus an 0-6-0 and a WD 2-8-0.

358. Lined up outside the shed—ex-L.N.E.R. K1 2-6-0 No. 62012 and three ex-North Eastern engines, Q6 0-8-0 No. 63346, J27 0-6-0 No. 65855 and Q6 0-8-0 No. 63437.

SUNDERLAND
(Ex-North Eastern Railway).

359. Two ex-N.E.R. J27 0-6-0s, Nos. 65789 and 65817, standing inside the shed.

BESCOT
(Ex-London & North Western Railway)

360. Ex-L & N.W.R. 0-8-0 No. 49361, and two ex-L.M.S. engines, 2-6-0 No. 46457 and 4F 0-6-0 No. 44448.

361. A general view of the shed.

WOODFORD HALSE
(Ex-Great Central Railway).

362. Ex-L.N.E.R. K3 2-6-0 No. 61960.

363. Ex-L.N.E.R. B1 4-6-0 No. 61368. Behind her stands another K3 2-6-0, No. 61843.

364. Basking in the sunshine outside Swindon shed on a Sunday afternoon in early autumn, 1959, two B.R. 9F 2-10-0s Nos. 92210 and 92212 and "Castle" class 4-6-0 No. 5058 "Earl of Clancarty". Standing between the 9Fs is a visitor, ex-L.N.E.R. B1 4-6-0 No. 61106 which had worked in a train from Banbury.

SWINDON.
(Ex-Great Western Railway).

366. A group of small ex-G.W.R. tank engines clustered round one of the turntables inside Swindon shed—0-4-2Ts Nos. 1462 and 1422, and 0-6-0 Pannier Tanks Nos. 4651, 6716 and 3653.

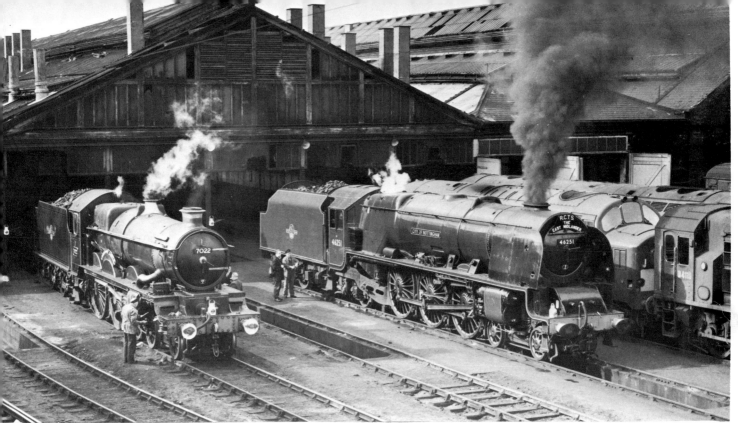

VISITING PACIFICS.

◄ **365.** Two famous engines, the ex-L.N.E.R. Pacific "Mallard" and the ex-G.W.R. 4-6-0 "King George V", standing side by side outside Swindon shed in pouring rain on 17th March, 1963. "Mallard" holds the world's record speed for a steam locomotive of 126 m.p.h.

367. One of the magnificent ex-L.M.S. Stanier Pacifics, No. 46251 "City of Nottingham", on Swindon shed prior to taking over an enthusiasts' special on 9th May, 1964. Standing alongside her is ex-G.W.R. "Castle" class 4-6-0 No. 7022 "Hereford Castle".

368. Another interesting visitor—ex-L.N.E.R. Pacific No. 4472 "Flying Scotsman" being serviced on Swindon shed during the course of working an enthusiasts' special on 17th August, 1964.

369. Southern array outside Salisbury shed. "West Country" Pacific No. 34099 "Lynmouth", S15 4-6-0 No. 30827, H15 4-6-0 No. 30522 and U 2-6-0 No. 31804.

SALISBURY
(Ex-London & South Western Railway).

Southern Elegance — "Merchant Navy" class Pacific No. 35026 "Lamport & Holt Line".

370. The view from the steps outside the foreman's office. The locomotive is S15 4-6-0 No. 30828.

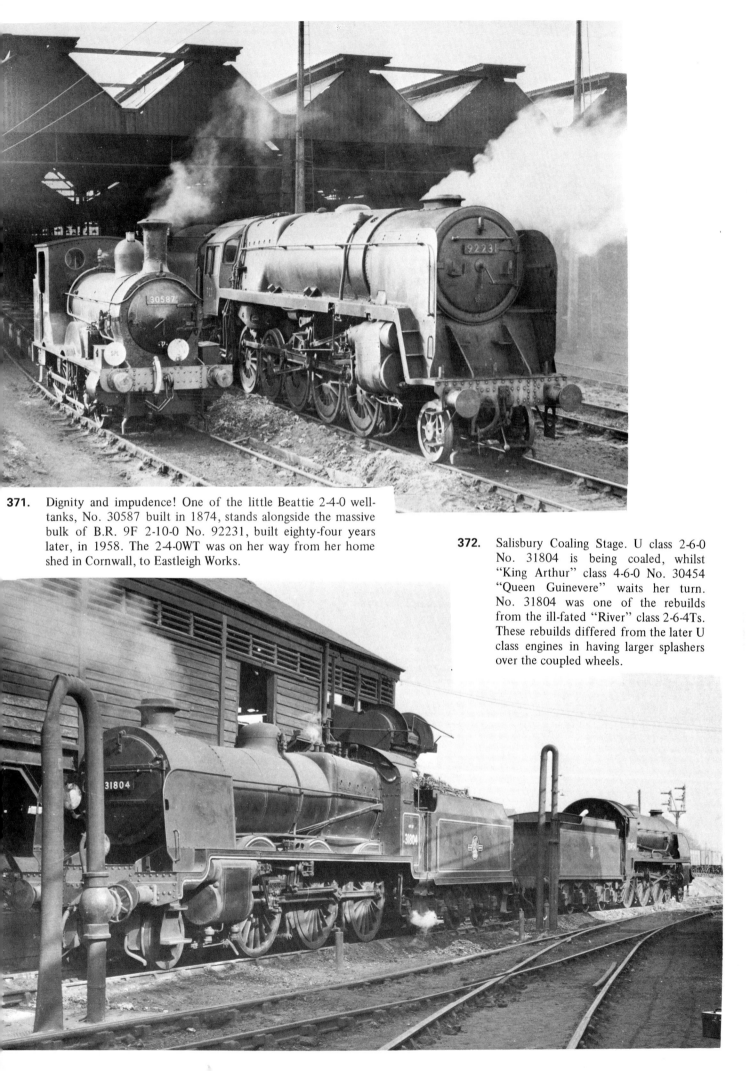

371. Dignity and impudence! One of the little Beattie 2-4-0 well-tanks, No. 30587 built in 1874, stands alongside the massive bulk of B.R. 9F 2-10-0 No. 92231, built eighty-four years later, in 1958. The 2-4-0WT was on her way from her home shed in Cornwall, to Eastleigh Works.

372. Salisbury Coaling Stage. U class 2-6-0 No. 31804 is being coaled, whilst "King Arthur" class 4-6-0 No. 30454 "Queen Guinevere" waits her turn. No. 31804 was one of the rebuilds from the ill-fated "River" class 2-6-4Ts. These rebuilds differed from the later U class engines in having larger splashers over the coupled wheels.

373. Three ex-Great Western 4-6-0s lined up outside the shed — No. 7033 "Hartlebury Castle", No. 6986 "Rydal Hall" and No. 1009 "County of Carmarthen". It is interesting to compare this view, taken in 1959, with picture 14, taken outside the old shed thirty-four years earlier, in 1925. "County" class engines appear in both pictures; in 1925 it is one of Churchward's 4-4-0s, introduced in 1904, whilst in this 1959 shot, the engine is a Hawksworth 4-6-0, built in 1946.

BRISTOL, BATH ROAD.
(Ex-Great Western Railway).

In 1933/4 the original shed and coaling stage at Bath Road had been demolished and replaced by an entirely new depot built on the site of the old Bristol & Exeter Railway Works, which had adjoined the old shed on the west side.

With the phasing out of steam traction on the Western Region, Bath Road shed was closed to steam locomotives in the autumn of 1960, and completely rebuilt as a modern diesel depot.

374. No. 5040, "Stokesay Castle", being coaled.

375. — and No. 7033, "Hartlebury Castle", being turned.

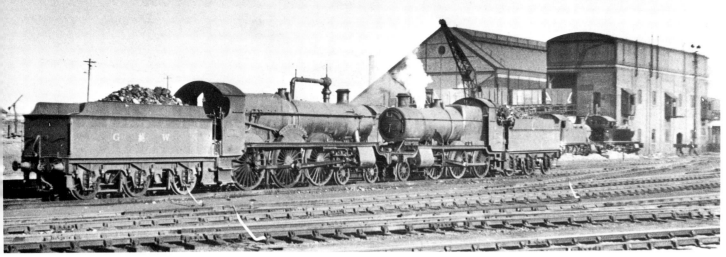

376. Bath Road in Great Western days — "Saint" class 4-6-0 No. 2941 "Easton Court", and a 43XX class 2-6-0.

377. A study in chimneys — "Castle", "Hall" and "County".

378. Two of the Beyer Peacock 2-4-0Ts, No.13 "Kissack" (1910) and No.12 "Hutchinson" (1908) standing in the terminus at Douglas. "Hutchinson" was preparing to leave shortly with the 11.45a.m. for Port Erin on 29th June, 1961.

THE ISLE OF MAN RAILWAY*
GAUGE: 3ft. 0in.

I have always had a fascination for narrow gauge railways. The outstanding system in the British Isles was the Isle of Man Railway, and for years I had wanted to visit this delightful 3ft. gauge line, but had been put off from doing so because I had heard that the management were against their line being photographed.

One evening in January, 1961, a friend of mine who held a senior executive position in British Railways, came to dinner and to see my 1960 "crop" of 16mm. films. When the viewing was over, he said, "And where are you planning to go this summer?" To which I replied that I longed to film the Isle of Man Railway, but I gathered that, unlike British Railways, they did not grant photographic permits. "Oh", said my B.R. friend, "I don't think that should present much of a problem. I will get our P.R.O. to contact Mr. Bond, Head of the Isle of Man Tourist Board. I am sure we can get things fixed up for you".

And so it came about that one morning in June, 1961, accompanied by my friend Norman Lockett, I set sail from Liverpool for Douglas in the Isle of Man, where I was to call on Mr. Bond who would introduce me to Mr. Sheard, general manager of the I.O. M.R. Mr. Bond gave us a very warm welcome and promptly took us round to the headquarters of the railway, where we were told that Mr. Sheard was not yet back from lunch. However, Mr. Sheard's assistant appeared on the scene asking if he could help, and when Mr. Bond explained the purpose of our visit, the immediate reply was, "Oh, that's impossible. Mr. Sheard *never* grants permission for *any* photography". My heart sank!

It was a glorious, hot summer's afternoon and so, whilst waiting for the return of Mr. Sheard, we all adjourned to a bar in the station forecourt to refresh ourselves. However, no sooner had we sat down when an elderly, distinguished looking gentleman passed by the open doorway. "Mr. Sheard!" called out our I.O.M.R. friend, and jumping to his feet, ushered in the general manager of the Isle of Man Railway. As soon as he was comfortably seated, and armed with a glass of light ale, Mr. Sheard turned towards Mr. Bond and said, "And what is the purpose of this meeting?" Mr. Bond answered, "Mr. Peters, and his friend Mr. Lockett, are over from the mainland and would much appreciate it if you would allow them to photograph the railway." There was a short pause, then came the sharp reply, "Oh no; quite out of the question; I never allow photography"—and then, turning suddenly to his assistant, barked,

"Do I?" "No, sir", came the instant reply, "That's what I told them sir." "But", interjected Mr. Bond, "these gentlemen are recommended by British Railways". I thought Mr. Sheard was going to do himself an injury! Purple in the face, he suddenly exploded, "This is *NOT* British Railways. This is the Isle of Man Railway of which I am general manager." His clenched fist came down on the table with a tremendous bang. All five glasses took off vertically to a height of at least half an inch, before crash-landing back on to the marbletopped table. "Permission refused!" Another tremendous bang on the table, and another instant take-off by the glasses.

The silence which followed seemed interminable. I stared glumly at the floor, thinking what an awful long way I had come for apparently nothing. Then Mr. Sheard spoke sharply to his assistant. "Well, haven't you got any work to do?"—Exit in a hurry, the assistant. Mr. Bond also rose to his feet, saying he had another appointment, and bade us farewell;—we were left alone with the still simmering Mr. Sheard. We finished our drinks and I asked Mr. Sheard if he would like another half pint—but the answer was no, so I got Norman Lockett's and my glasses replenished, thinking that at least we might try and drown our sorrows a little. Then I turned to Mr. Sheard and said "It is our first visit to the Island; are you sure you won't join us?"—and somewhat to my surprise, this produced the response, "Well, just a half then."

Outside the sunshine streamed down in the forecourt, and in the distance we could hear faintly the whistling of the little engines as they went about their duties. Misery surrounded me! Then, half way through his second drink, Mr. Sheard suddenly put down his glass and said, "What exactly was it that you wanted to do, Mr. Peters?" I explained how I had hoped to film his line. There was a long pause, then Mr. Sheard stood up, "Well, I don't see why that shouldn't be arranged. Come with me!"

From that moment on, Mr. Sheard could not do enough for us. We were introduced to Mr. Shaw the locomotive superintendent, the station foreman, and other members of the staff. To all, Mr. Sheard said, "These are two of my friends over from the mainland. They have come to film the railway. Please give them every assistance and co-operation."

All I need add is that the next few days were some of the happiest and most successful narrow gauge filming sessions I ever had.

Profusely illustrated in my book "The Narrow Gauge Charm of Yesterday" published by the Oxford Publishing Co.

LONGLEAT.
GAUGE: 1ft. 3in.

379. Several of the Stately Homes of England which are open to the public, have miniature passenger-carrying lines. A splendid little railway, operated by a mixed stud of diminutive steam and diesel locomotives, has been laid in the grounds of the Marquis of Bath's estate at Longleat in Wiltshire. In 1970, two of the steam locomotives were "Dougal" and "Muffin", seen here running round the loop in the woods at the far end of the line.

BICTON
GAUGE: 1ft. 6in.

380. 0-4-0T. "Woolwich" emerging from a leafy grove on the Bicton Woodland Railway. This delightful line runs through the very beautiful grounds of Bicton Gardens, near East Budleigh, Devon. Because of the unusual gauge of 1ft. 6in., there is at present, only one steam locomotive on the line, "Woolwich", built by Avonside in 1916, maker's number 1748.

381. 0-4-2ST, No. 4 "Edward Thomas" standing at Abergynolwyn in June, 1956, with a train composed of both open and closed coaches. No. 4 is an ex-Corris Railway engine built by Kerr Stuart in 1921, maker's number 4047.

382. 0-4-0WT No. 6 "Douglas", Andrew Barclay, 1431/1918, about to set off from Towyn with a train for Abergynolwyn in the summer of 1963.

TWO WELL-KNOWN PRESERVED LINES IN   NORTH WALE

THE TALYLLYN RAILWAY
GAUGE: 2ft. 3in.

383.

In the autumn of 1957, Mr. A.G.W. Garraway, general manager of the Festiniog Railway, is propelled past Boston Lodge by 0-4-0ST. "Prince", built by George England in 1863.

THE FESTINIOG RAILWAY.
GAUGE: 1ft. 11½in.

384. "Linda", rounding "Whistling Curve" with her train, draws near to Tan-y-Bwlch in the summer of 1970. "Linda" and her sister "Blanche" — see picture 391 — were built by Hunslet for the Penrhyn Railway in 1893; their maker's numbers are 590 and 589. Since being bought by the Festiniog Railway, both engines have been rebuilt with a leading ponytruck and converted to oil firing.

385. 2-6-2T. No. 9 "Prince of Wales", built by Davies & Metcalfe in 1902, climbing toward Devil's Bridge with the 2.15p.m. from Aberystwyth in June, 1970. As the railway climbs higher and higher up the Rheidol Valley, the view from the train becomes increasingly magnificent — far better than can be seen from the nearby main road.

THE VALE OF RHEIDOL RAILWAY
GAUGE: 1ft. 11½in.

◁ During the climb from Aberystwyth up to Devil's Bridge, all trains stop at Aber-Ffrwd for the engine to take water.

THE WELSHPOOL & LLANFAIR RAILWAY
GAUGE: 2ft. 6in.

386. The two original Welshpool & Llanfair locomotives 0-6-0Ts, "The Earl" and "The Countess", built by Beyer Peacock in 1902, maker's numbers 3496 and 3497.

387. "The Earl" crossing over the road at Castle Caereinion. (See also picture 436).

388. Three of the Bowater locomotives — 0-6-2Ts, "Triumph", Bagnall 2511/1934, and "Superior", Kerr Stuart 4034/1920, and 0-4-2ST "Premier", Kerr Stuart 886/1905.

PAPER MILLS —

THE BOWATER RAILWAY
GAUGE: 2ft. 6in.

Until 1969 Bowater's United Kingdom Paper Mills Ltd., operated an extensive narrow gauge railway linking their mills at Sittingbourne and Kemsley with Ridham Dock. After the system ceased to be used commercially, the Company leased a part of the line to the Locomotive Club of Great Britain, and over this section, passenger-carrying trains are run during the summer season.

389. 0-6-2T. "Superb", Bagnall 2684/1940.

390. 0-6-2T. "Chevallier", Manning Wardle 1877/1915.

PENRHYN SLATE QUARRIES*

GAUGE: 1ft. 10¾in

391

An extensive narrow gauge tramway system served these very large quarries, and the company also operated a 6½ mile-long 1ft. 10¾in. gauge "mainline" linking the quarries at Bethesda, with Port Penrhyn. Three 0-4-0 saddle-tanks, of rather larger proportions than the quarry engines, worked the "main-line". All three were built by Hunslet, "Charles" in 1882, and the twins "Blanche" and "Linda" in 1893. I used to make regular pilgrimages to North Wales, and took this picture of "Blanche" approaching the quarries at Bethesda in June 1956.

"Charles" is now in Penrhyn Castle Museum, whilst "Blanche" and "Linda", both considerably altered, are running on the Festiniog Railway. (See picture 384).

SLATE QUARRIES.

To anyone with a love of very small engines, the slate quarries of North Wales were a Seventh Heaven, for they teemed with diminutive steam locomotives.

DINORWIC SLATE QUARRIES*

GAUGE: 1ft 10¾in.

392.

The vast Dinorwic slate quarries at Llanberis employed a host of delightful little 0-4-0 saddle-tanks. All but three were built by Hunslet, and in this picture, one of the "odd girls out", "Sybil", Bagnall 1760/1906, is standing beside one of the Hunslets, "George B", 680/1898.

*Profusely illustrated in my book "The Narrow Gauge Charm of Yesterday", published by the Oxford Publishing Co.

393. 0-6-0ST "Kettering Furnace No. 8", Manning Wardle 1675/1906, trundles along the edge of a field as she wends her way through the countryside with a load of iron ore.

IRONSTONE TRAMWAYS.

Quarrying for ironstone used to be carried out very extensively in the Midlands of England. Many of the quarries had their own railway system, and of these, four were narrow gauge lines worked by steam locomotives.

EATON QUARRIES (WALTHAM)

GAUGE: 1 METRE.

394.

Amongst the engines that worked this line were two French-built locomotives. This is 0-6-0T "Nantes", built by Veuve Corpet & L. Louvet in 1903, maker's number 936.

SCALDWELL QUARRIES*
GAUGE: 3ft. 0in.

395. "Lamport", an 0-6-0ST built by Peckett in 1913, maker's number 1315, plods uphill with a string of small wooden wagons laden with iron ore.

EASTWELL QUARRIES.
GAUGE: 3ft. 0in.

396. A most interesting "mixed bag" of locomotives worked this line. Standing outside their shed are 0-4-0ST. "Underbank", Peckett 873/1900, and 0-6-0ST. "Belvoir", Hunslet 1823/1936.

*Profusely illustrated in my book "The Narrow Gauge Charm of Yesterday", published by the Oxford Publishing Co.

GROUDLE GLEN
GAUGE: 2ft. 0in.

397. At Groudle Glen, to the east of Onchan in the Isle of Man, a 2 foot gauge passenger-carrying line used to be worked by two attractive little 2-4-0 side-tanks. Standing with her two-coach train is "Polar Bear", built by Bagnall in 1906, maker's number 1781.

CADEBY
GAUGE: 2ft. 0in.

398. A scene on the Rev. Teddy Boston's Cadeby Light Railway, which is laid in the grounds of Cadeby Rectory. The Rev. Teddy Boston looks out happily from the cab, as his 0-4-0ST. "Pixie", Bagnall 2090/1919, passes by with a staff special.

IMPERIAL SMELTING CORPORATION
GAUGE: 2ft. 0in.

399. The Imperial Smelting Corporation used to operate a 2 foot gauge line within the confines of their large plant at Avonmouth. This picture of their last surviving narrow gauge steam locomotive, an 0-4-0ST built by Kerr Stuart in 1918, maker's number 3128, was taken in 1955 shortly before the engine was withdrawn from service.

JOURNEY'S END

400. In the early summer of 1958, a small 2 foot gauge locomotive owned by Roads Reconstruction Ltd. — Andrew Barclay 0-4-0WT, 1855/1931 — sits quietly in a field at Cranmore, awaiting her fate. Shortly after this picture was taken, she was scrapped.

401. In the summer of 1951, an up express comes in past Bath's wooden bracket signal dating back to Midland Railway days. The train is the 9.25a.m. (SO) Bournemouth to Manchester and Liverpool, hauled by 2P 4-4-0 No. 40700 and Stanier class 5 4-6-0 No. 44826.

ENGINEERING WORK.

Bath's old Midland Railway wooden bracket signal is replaced by a new signal fabricated from steel.

402. Sunday morning, 3rd June, 1956. Final adjustments are made to the new signal, lying on the ground prior to erection.

403. After the old wooden signal had been felled, it was broken up where it lay, and loaded piecemeal into a waiting wagon. The crane then raised the new signal into position.

TURNTABLE TROUBLES AT BATH

The periodic non-availability of Bath's turntable produced major headaches for the operating department, for whenever the turntable was unserviceable, the only way engines could be turned was by running them ten miles up the Midland line to the triangle junction at Mangotsfield.

404.

Bath's turntable being renewed in December, 1950.

405. Whilst being overhauled in April, 1953, Bath's turntable was out of action for a week. Engines arriving at Bath off the Somerset & Dorset line, were coupled together, four or five at a time, and run as a "Train of engines" up to Mangotsfield to turn. This "train" of five engines off the S & D, turning at Mangotsfield on 11th April, consists of Stanier class 5 4-6-0 No. 44965, two S & D 7F 2-8-0s Nos. 53809 and 53802 and two S.R. Pacifics, No. 34042 "Dorchester" and No. 34040 "Crewkerne".

PLATFORM RENEWAL AT SALTFORD.

406.

In the spring of 1951, the wooden extensions of both platforms at the eastern end of Saltford station, were replaced by more substantial structures of brick and pre-cast concrete slabs. Intensive work was put in over several Sundays, necessitating single-line working. A down express, hauled by No. 6986 "Rydal Hall", passes through cautiously on the up road.

407.
On 24th April, 1953, S.R. "Merchant Navy" Pacific No. 35020 fractured her driving axle whilst passing through Crewkerne at speed. As a result, all thirty engines of the class were withdrawn for examination, and several locomotives were borrowed from other Regions during the emergency. Passing through Crewkerne on 23rd May with the third portion of the down "Atlantic Coast Express" is V2 2-6-2 No. 60928, which was on loan from the Eastern Region.

UNUSUAL POWER ON THE SOUTHERN WEST-OF-ENGLAND MAIN LINE.

408. Early in 1965, a sudden but temporary shortage of DMUs in the West Country, led to two small ex-Great Western 0-4-2Ts being hastily borrowed from Yeovil Shed in order to work the Seaton branch for a short while. Coupled together, Nos. 1442 and 1450 travelled west down the Southern main-line on Sunday, 7th February. At Axminster both engines took water, with No. 1442 slightly over-judging things!

CENTENARY CELEBRATIONS

09. The Somerset Central Railway was opened between Glastonbury and Highbridge on 28th August, 1854, and to celebrate the centenary, a special train was run from Glastonbury over to Burnham-on-Sea on 28th August, 1954. The engine chosen to haul the train was 3F 0-6-0 No. 43201, which had been built for the Somerset & Dorset at Derby in 1896. In this picture of the 3F setting off with her train, Glastonbury Tor may just be discerned on the skyline above the engine.

410. To commemorate the centenary of the Salisbury – Exeter line, a celebration was held at Exeter Central Station on 19th July, 1960. Beattie 2-4-0WT No. 30587, with the ex-L & S.W.R. two-car "Gate" set off the Yeovil Town branch, and a third coach, made the short journey from St. James Park Halt into Exeter Central. The engine crew and the passengers were dressed in period costume for the occasion.

FILM MAKING — "THE TITFIELD THUNDERBOLT".

This comedy film was made in 1952 on the old G.W.R. Limpley Stoke — Camerton branch. The star performer — and working under her own steam — was the wonderful old 0-4-2 "Lion", built for the Liverpool and Manchester Railway in 1838 by Todd, Kitson and Laird.

411. "Lion" sitting in Monkton Combe yard shortly after arriving on the branch in June, 1952.

412. For the film, "Lion" was temporarily rechristened "Thunderbolt". She is seen here standing beside a dummy "film set" water tower. Water for "Thunderbolt" was in fact obtained from the stream in the background via a portable pump.

413. "Thunderbolt" pauses briefly with her train beneath an overbridge near the village of Combe Hay.

A BRITISH RAILWAYS FILM ON EMERGENCY SINGLE-LINE WORKING.

In 1956 British Railways decided to produce, for staff training, an instructional film on Emergency Single-line Working. Because, after the end of the summer service, no trains ran on Sundays between Bath and Evercreech Junction, the Somerset and Dorset line was selected for the making of the film, and this took place on Sundays in September and October.

As the film was intended for showing throughout B.R., considerable pains were taken to try and prevent it from being identified with any particular Region. Shepton Mallet and Binegar, the two stations which appeared in the film, had their names changed; Binegar became "Boiland" and Shepton Mallet, "Averton Hammer". For passenger trains the engines used were B.R. standard class 4 and class 5 4-6-0s – types which could have been seen anywhere on B.R. However, when it came to filming the goods train scenes, the cat was well and truly let out of the bag, for the engine used was one of the highly individual S & D 7F 2-8-0s!

414. The director of the B.T.C. Film Unit, Mr. Fairbairn (arms raised) gives some final instructions to the driver before the filming of a "setting back" sequence.

415.

Filming a banked, north-bound goods. One camera crew were on the bank engine, 3F 0-6-0 No. 43194, whilst the train was also being filmed from the motorised platelayers' trolley, coming up astern on the other road.

416.

A close-up of the camera crew on the bank engine as she passed by.

417. Midland Railway 4-2-2 No. 118, designed by S.W. Johnson and built at Derby in 1897.

THE BEAUTY OF A BYGONE AGE

Four preserved engines from pre-grouping days.

418. Midland Railway 2-4-0 No. 158A, designed by Matthew Kirtley and built in 1866.

419. The famous Caledonian Single No. 123, built in 1886, which took part in the races to Edinburgh in 1888.

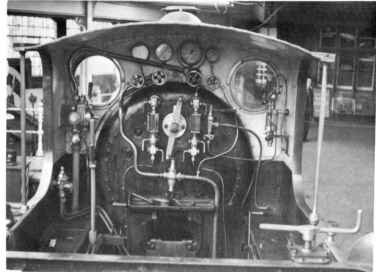

420. The cab of Caledonian Single No. 123.

421.

London & South Western Railway Adams T3 4-4-0 No. 563, built in 1893. Behind her stands the preserved Midland — Glasgow and South Western Joint Stock twelve-wheeled dining car.

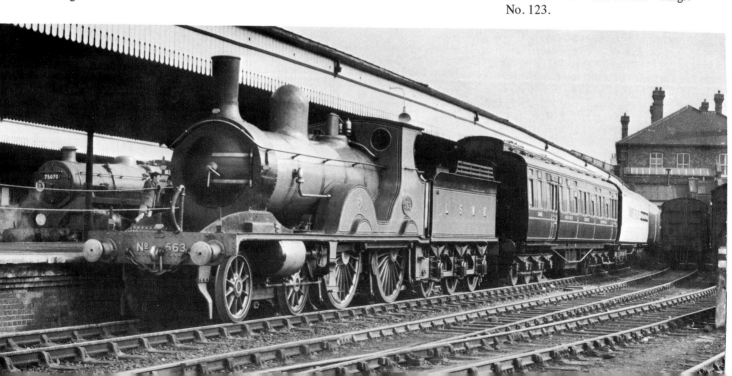

CRANE PREDICAMENT.

In 1933 a start was made on a programme of bridge strengthening on the Midland line between Mangotsfield and Bath, to permit heavier and more powerful locomotives to work down to Bath, and on over the Somerset and Dorset line.

On Sunday afternoon, 27th August, 1933, I was visiting my godfather, whose home at Twerton, on the western outskirts of Bath, overlooked the Midland line. Suddenly we heard the faint sound of much shouting and general commotion coming from the railway, and on going into the garden to investigate, we saw that a crane, trying to lift a heavy bridge girder, had been pulled over by the weight of the girder, and was poised on the brink of disaster! By great good fortune, no one was hurt in the mishap.

422. The L.M.S. crane, tilted over at a precarious angle. Fortunately the bridge girder caught the platform of the crane and prevented it from toppling into the roadway below.

Drama

423.

In the early evening, the G.W.R. breakdown crane from Bristol arrived on the scene and rescued the L.M.S. crane from its predicament. In the foreground is the girder which caused the trouble. When the accident happened, it had crashed into the roadway below and broken in two.

G.W.R. 2-6-2T No. 5527
BURSTS A STEAM PIPE.

On 22nd August, 1953, I was driving towards Saltford along the main road which runs parallel with the railway when I began to overhaul a down local train, preparing to stop at the station. Suddenly a great volume of steam gushed from the locomotive's cab, and the next moment the fireman leapt from the engine. A steam pipe had burst in the cab, but almost miraculously, neither the driver nor the fireman was seriously hurt, although both had been forced to jump from the engine whilst it was still in motion.

424. After a commendably short time, Pannier Tank No. 7718, sent to the rescue from Bristol, arrived on the scene and removed No. 5527 from her train.

425. With the 2-6-2T. safely removed to Saltford's small goods yard, No. 5970 "Hengrave Hall" passes by with an up express, watched by my son Julian.

426.
The Pannier Tank then took No. 5527's train on to Bristol, whilst the local fire brigade turned up to put out the fire in the disabled locomotive.

427. Over the years, many interesting locomotives were used on the Longmoor Military Railway. In this picture, 2-10-0 No. 600 "Gordon", absolutely immaculate in blue livery, is drawing near to Liss Forest with a train from Liss to Longmoor Downs.

LONGMOOR MILITARY RAILWAY.

For training Army personnel in all aspects of railway construction, maintenance and running, the War Department operated an extensive system at Longmoor in Hampshire. At regular intervals, the Army would hold an "Open Day", when members of the public were allowed to visit this most interesting railway.

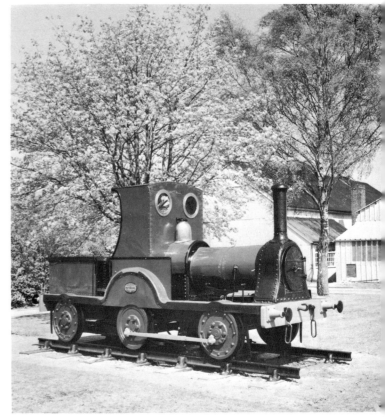

428. This amusing little ex-Shropshire and Montgomeryshire Railway 0-4-2, "Gazelle" — looking like a child's toy — was preserved outside the main administrative block. She was built by Dodman of Lynn in 1893, starting off life as a 2-2-2 well-tank, and being converted to an 0-4-2 in 1911.

429.
The L.M.R. operated several "Austerity" 0-6-0STs. No. 196 is standing at Longmoor Downs with a train for Bordon.

430. A picture taken from the cab of B.R. standard class '5' No. 73047 as, with 2P 4-4-0 No. 40634 working hard ahead of her, she laboured up the northern slopes of the Mendip hills with the down "Pines Express" in June, 1956. The two engines had already covered some five miles, much of it at 1 in 50, during the course of the climb from Radstock, and still had a further two and a half miles to go, before they would reach Masbury Summit, 811 feet above sea level.

FROM THE INSIDE, LOOKING OUT.

Just occasionally I had the great good fortune to be granted the privilege of a footplate permit, and so had the opportunity of having a go at taking pictures from an engine.

431.

In May, 1961, I was allowed to ride in the driver's cab of the "Blue Pullman" from Bath up to Paddington. Approaching Didcot at high speed, we met a "Castle" proceeding westwards, equally rapidly, with a down express.

432. The engine of an enthusiasts' special invariably carried a head board. Sometimes this could be a little over-powering —

PART 14
Enthusiasts' Specials

These trains did not really start coming into prominence until the mid-fifties. As steam began to disappear from British Railways, so more and more enthusiasts' specials were run and — a pleasing feature — invariably they would be hauled by a clean locomotive.

433. — and then possibly the best thing was to try a "going away" shot. These two pictures of ex-G.W.R. 4-4-0 No. 3440 "City of Truro" were taken at Bath in the early evening of 15th June 1957.

434.
Ex-L & S.W.R. B4 0-4-0T No. 30096 standing in Winchester, Chesil, station on 6th April, 1963, with a special organised by the Locomotive Club of Great Britain. In contrast to some boards, the L.C.G.B. head-board is a model of neatness and good taste.

'LAST TRAINS".

435. The remote Cromford and High Peak line came to an end in April, 1967. On the last day, Sunday, 30th April, a Stephenson Locomotive Society special composed of several brakevans hauled by two "austerity" 0-6-0STs Nos. 68006 and 68012, ran between Middleton Top and Friden. In this picture Nos. 68006 and 68012, on a return run from Friden to Middleton Top, have just negotiated the very sharp curve at Gotham. At 8 a.m. the next morning, work commenced on lifting the track.

436. A head-board that happily turned out to be incorrect! In 1956 British Railways decided to close the narrow gauge Welshpool and Llanfair Light Railway, and on 3rd November an S.L.S. "Farewell" special ran over the line. This is the scene at Castle Caereinion where the train had drawn in to the sounds of the Dead March in Saul played by the Newtown Silver Band.

As is well known, the story has a happy ending, for the railway was saved by the Welshpool & Llanfair Light Railway Preservation Society who are now running this attractive little line with great success.

437.

On 25th August, 1956, a special train was run for the S.L.S. to celebrate the centenary of the opening of the branch to Dursley. In addition to traversing the Dursley branch, the special ran up the branch lines to Stroud, Nailsworth and Thornbury, all of which had been closed to passenger traffic for some years. To eliminate "running-round" difficulties, the three-coach train was worked by an engine at both ends. Setting off from Nailsworth, old Midland Railway 0-6-0T No. 41748 was at the leading end, whilst out of sight, trailing at the rear, was Ivatt 2-6-2T No. 41208.

BRANCH LINE VISITS.

438. On Sunday, 5th April, 1964, the last day of the Tetbury branch, ex-G.W.R. 0-4-2T No. 1472 sets off from Tetbury for Kemble with a special organised by the Gloucestershire Railway Society.

439. Two Ivatt 2-6-2Ts, Nos, 41301 and 41284, nearing Corfe Castle with a Locomotive Club of Great Britain special over the Swanage branch on 27th February, 1966.

SMALL TANK ENGINES IN DOUBLE-HARNESS.

440.

The "South Western Limited", a special tour train organised by the Southern Counties Touring Society, climbing up hill near Budleigh Salterton on 2nd September, 1962, hauled by two ex-L & S.W.R. M7 0-4-4Ts Nos. 30025 and 30024.

441. The "Farnborough Flyer", drawn by the preserved G.N.R. Atlantic No. 251 and ex-G.C.R. 4-4-0 No. 62663 "Prince Albert", arriving at Basingstoke.

ROYAL OBSERVER CORPS SPECIAL

On 12th September, 1954, Mr. Alan Pegler organised a special train, "The Farnborough Flyer", to take members of the Royal Observer Corps from Leeds to Farnborough for the annual Air Display. From Leeds as far as Basingstoke, the train was hauled by the preserved G.N.R. Atlantic No. 251 and G.C.R. 4-4-0 No. 62663 "Prince Albert". The ex-L.N.E.R. beaver-tail car was on the end of the train.

442.
The two engines, and a "King Arthur" 4-6-0, on shed at Basingstoke. On the right is the ex-L.N.E.R. beaver-tail car.

443.
The preserved G.N.R. Atlantic No. 251 standing beside ex-S.R. "Schools" class 4-4-0 No. 30901 "Winchester".

444. The graceful Midland compound, No. 1000, running between Wixford and Alcester with a Gloucestershire Railway Society special on 27th May, 1961.

TWO PRESERVED 4-4-0s.

445. The famous Great Western 4-4-0 No. 3440 "City of Truro" setting off from Temple Meads, Bristol, on 19th May, 1957, with a special excursion train to South Devon.

SPECIALS IN SCOTLAND.

446. The Caledonian single No. 123, with two restored Caledonian coaches, near Auchengray on 19th April, 1965.

447. Ex-Caledonian Railway 0-6-0 No. 57375 arriving at Garlieston from Millisle, on the Whithorn branch, with an enthusiasts' special on 15th April, 1963.

48. The preserved Great North of Scotland Railway 4-4-0 No. 49 "Gordon Highlander", setting off from Auchengray with a three-coach special on 16th October, 1965.

449. The scene on 17th April, 1965, as the preserved Highland Railway "Jones Goods" 4-6-0 No. 103 climbs away from Upper Port Glasgow in the early evening with an enthusiasts' special.

BLUEBELL SPECIALS.

450. Captain W.G. Smith's preserved Great Northern Railway 0-6-0ST No. 247 stops at Three Bridges for water whilst hauling the "Blue Belle" special from London to the Bluebell Railway on 1st April, 1962.

451. In the autumn of 1962, another "Blue Belle" special was run from London down to the Bluebell Railway. This time the train was hauled by the preserved L & S.W.R. T9 4-4-0 No. 120, seen here arriving at Haywards Heath on 21st October, 1962.

TALYLLYN SPECIALS.

452. Each year a special train is run from London to Towyn for the A.G.M. of the Talyllyn Railway Preservation Society. In 1957 the motive power for the train west of Shrewsbury was ex-Lancashire and Yorkshire Railway 2-4-2T No. 50781 and ex-G.W.R. 4-4-0 No. 9021, pictured here between Montgomery and Abermule.

453.

In 1956 the Talyllyn special had been hauled from Shrewsbury to Towyn by ex-South Eastern and Chatham Railway Wainwright 4-4-0 No. 31075 and ex-G.W.R. Dean 0-6-0 No. 2538. In this picture they are climbing towards Talerddig Summit.

454. On 3rd July, 1966, a special train was run for the L.C.G.B. from London to Weymouth. In this picture, ex-L.M.S. Stanier class 5 No. 45493 and ex-S.R. Bulleid Pacific No. 34006 "Salisbury" are climbing the bank out of Weymouth with the special on the return run to London.

455. The restored Great Western 4-6-0 No. 4079 "Pendennis Castle" heading east from Sapperton tunnel with an Ian Allan Rail Tour special on 8th August, 1965.

456. The preserved L.N.E.R. 2-6-0 No. 3442 "The Great Marquess" running north from Worcester with an S.L.S. special on 19th September, 1965.

457. An ex-L.N.E.R. A4 Pacific in the West Country. No. 60024 "Kingfisher", hauling an A4 Preservation Society special, draws near to Milborne Port on the Southern West-of-England main line on 26th March, 1966.

458.
An early taste of diesel. Diesel railcars were pioneered by the Great Western Railway, the first units being introduced in 1934; this car, No. W24W was built in 1940. No. W24W, seen standing in Bath, Green Park, station on 20th April, 1954, was to form the 10.00 a.m. to Bristol.

PART 15
Non Steam

459. Diesel luxury. The down Bristol "Blue Pullman" leaves Twerton tunnel on 29th August, 1961. These diesel-electric Pullmans, introduced in 1959, were made up in trains of six-car and eight-car units, the end cars being Power Cars. The first appearance of a "Blue Pullman" on the Western Region was in 1960; on Tuesday, 6th September an inaugural run — on which I was privileged to be a guest — was made from Bristol to Reading and back. When new, or just out of shops, the riding of these trains was remarkably good, but unfortunately this rapidly deteriorated in service, and within a few weeks, reached a stage where the safe maximum contents for a cup of coffee, was half-full! The "Blue Pullmans" only had a short life, the last being withdrawn in 1973.

THE TWO WESTERN REGION GAS TURBINES.

460. In the early 'fifties the Western Region of
and B.R., carrying on the pioneering spirit of the
461. old G.W.R., was experimenting with two
most interesting gas turbine-electric locomotives. The first of these, A1A-A1A No.
18000, had in fact been ordered from
Brown, Boveri in Switzerland by the Great
Western just prior to nationalisation. On the
left is the maker's plate of No. 18000 and,
above, she is seen standing at the western
end of Bath Spa station with a down express
on 9th September, 1950.

462.

This is the second of the
Western Region's gas turbines,
built by Metropolitan Vickers
in 1950. She bore the number
18100, and in this picture is
passing through Sydney Gardens, Bath, with the down
"Merchant Venturer" on 19th
April, 1952.

463. Diesel-electric Co-Co No. 10000 climbing Parkstone bank, between Poole and Bournemouth, with an up train on 4th August, 1954. The 1600 h.p. No. 10000 and her sister No. 10001 were two of the pioneers of mainline diesel-electric traction in Britain. They were ordered by the L.M.S. and entered service just prior to nationalisation.

EARLY DIESELS.

464. In the late 'forties the Southern Railway also decided to try diesel-electric traction for main-line use, and ordered two 1750 h.p. 1 Co-Co 1 locomotives. These were delivered in 1951, after the Southern Railway had been nationalised, and became B.R. Nos. 10201 and 10202. This is No. 10201 passing Holes Bay Junction with an up express on 3rd August, 1954.

DIESEL PROTOTYPES.

466. Another contender for the type 4 specification was Co-Co No. D0280 "Falcon", built by Brush. This is "Falcon" passing through Sydney Gardens, Bath, with the 1.45p.m. down express from Paddington on 26th March, 1968.

465. B.R., having decided to eliminate steam traction completely, drew up specifications for a series of standard diesel-electric type locomotives of varying horse power. Several manufacturers built prototypes for consideration by B.R. A contender for the type 4 specification of 2700 h.p., was Co-Co No. D0260, "Lion", a joint project by BRCW–AEI–Sulzer. "Lion" was painted white and whilst on test, was kept in immaculate condition by her manufacturers. On 24th July, 1962, she worked a test train of sixteen coaches down the Western Region main line to Bristol and is seen here approaching Keynsham at 86 m.p.h. (official figure).

WESTERN REGION DIESEL-HYDRAULICS.

468. The initial batch of five "Warships" had the wheel formation A1A–A1A, but for the seventy-one engines that followed, this was modified to B–B. On 30th July, 1968, No. D831 "Monarch" and No. D808 "Centaur" set off from Westbury with the 2.30 p.m. Plymouth to Paddington.

467. Unlike all the other Regions of B.R., the Western Region decided to use diesel-hydraulic traction in preference to diesel-electric. The initial order for type 4s was for five A1A–A1A locomotives of 2000 h.p. to be built by the North British Locomotive Company. The first of these locomotives entered service in 1958 and, continuing an old Great Western practice, all were given names, the class being known as the "Warships". A comprehensive programme of testing was put in hand in the spring of 1958, and the second of the class, No. D601 "Ark Royal", is seen entering Stoke Gifford yard on 25th April after a test run from Reading. The Great Western dynamometer car is next to the engine.

On the left is No. 5940 "Whitbourne Hall" in charge of an Eastbound goods.

469. The largest diesel-hydraulic locomotives on the Western Region were the 2700 h.p. C–C "Western" class 52s introduced in 1961. "Westerns" were constructed at both Swindon and Crewe, the class eventually totalling seventy-four locomotives. In the summer of 1970, No. D1006 "Western Stalwart" arrives at Merehead Quarry with a train of empties.

470. The type 3 diesel-hydraulic used by the Western Region was the 1700 h.p. B–B "Hymek". One hundred and one of these locomotives were constructed by Beyer Peacock, the first entering service in 1961. On a warm summer's evening in 1968, No. D7039 is climbing towards Clutton, on the North Somerset line, with a train of empty coal wagons for the Radstock collieries.

DIESEL-ELECTRICS — TYPE 4.

471. One of the early Type 4 diesel-electrics on B.R. was the 1Co-Co1 "Peak" class of 2500 h.p., which entered service in 1959. In this picture a "Peak" in charge of a down express has just emerged from Blea Moor tunnel on the Settle and Carlisle line.

472. The most numerous of all Type 4 diesel-electric locomotives on B.R. are the Brush Co-Cos of classes 47 and 48. Introduced in 1962, over five hundred of these locomotives have been constructed. Nearing Bradford-on-Avon in June, 1967, is No. D1740 in charge of the 10.30a.m. Bristol to Eastleigh freight.

DIESEL-ELECTRICS — TYPE 3.

473. A pair of class 37 1750 h.p. Co-Co diesel-electric locomotives set off from Bath on 15th May, 1966 with the 12.45p.m. Paddington to Bristol. Three hundred and nine of these Type 3 locomotives have been built by the English Electric Company, the first entering service in 1961.

474. The Type 3 diesel-electric locomotives used on the Southern Region are mainly Bo—Bo classes 33 and 34 of 1550 h.p., ninety-eight of which have been built by the Birmingham R.C. & W. Company. Two of these Southern Type 3s, Nos. D6563 and D6575, are descending towards Buckhorn Weston tunnel in charge of the 8.50a.m. Brighton to Exeter on 27th July, 1968. As can be seen, by 1968 this once thriving mainline had been singled — (See picture 306).

DIESEL-ELECTRICS.

475. B.R. has a large number of Type 2 diesel-electric locomotives. No. D5355 — seen here at Grayrigg with an empty stock train one evening in late April, 1967 — is a member of class 27. These 1250 h.p., Bo—Bo locomotives were built by the Birmingham R.C. & W. Company, and first entered service in 1958.

476. One of the earliest Type 4 diesel-electrics to be introduced on B.R. were the 1Co-Co1 class 40 locomotives of 2000 h.p. The English Electric Company built two hundred of these locomotives, the first of which entered service in 1958. This is No. D318 leaving Crewe with the up Irish Mail on 30th June, 1961.

ELECTRICS.

478. One of the outstanding 3500 h.p. class 86 Bo—Bo electric locomotives, No. E3145, bursts out of Shugborough tunnel with an up express in May, 1972.

477. No. E6009 running through the New Forest east of Brockenhurst with an up express in July, 1967. Bo—Bo No. E6009 is one of the Southern Region's interesting Electro-Diesel locomotives. Normally these work from the 750 V.d.c. third rail supply when their h.p. is 1600. However, they are also capable of running where there is no third rail, for they are equipped with a diesel generator which supplies power for the traction motors, albeit at the reduced h.p. figure of 600.

THINGS TO COME......

AND A LAST GLIMPSE OF THE OLD SPLENDOUR

479. 1975—and the opening of a new era. The first of British Railway's new High Speed Trains (HST) sweeps eastwards towards Bath on a cold morning in early spring.

480. The Royal train glides away towards Westbury. B.R. have announced that the old stock of the Royal train is to be replaced with new vehicles of modern construction.